FROM FIJI TO BALKAN SKIES

First published in 2000 by
WOODFIELD PUBLISHING
Bognor Regis, West Sussex PO21 5EL, UK.

© Dennis McCaig, 2000

ISBN 0 873203 47 0

All rights reserved. No part of this publication
may be reproduced or transmitted in any form
or by any means, electronic or mechanical, nor
may it be stored in any information storage and
retrieval system, without prior permission
from the publisher.

FROM
Fiji to Balkan Skies

A Fighter Pilot's Memories of 249 Squadron, World War II

DENNIS 'FIJI' McCAIG

Woodfield Publishing

The Author, Flt/Lt Dennis McCaig, RAF Commissioned and Confident 1943.

Contents

Foreword 7
249 Squadron 9
Chapter 1 Into Action 16
Chapter 2 First Blood 23
Chapter 3 The Killing War 31
Chapter 4 Falling Down to Earth 48
Chapter 5 Survival 62
Chapter 6 Salvation 71
Chapter 7 Coming Down the Mountain 88
Chapter 8 Airlift to Safety 102
Chapter 9 Back to the War 126
Chapter 10 Red Leader 140
Chapter 11 Down to Earth Again 151
Chapter 12 The Rescue That Never Was 164
Chapter 13 Betrayed 181
Chapter 14 A Long Journey 193
Chapter 15 Companionship & Compassion 206
Chapter 16 Interrogation 214
Chapter 17 A Train Journey to Forget 222
Chapter 18 Incarceration 229
Chapter 19 The Long March 234
Chapter 20 Sweet Freedom 245

*The Author, Flt/Lt Dennis McCaig, RAF
Captured and confined, February 1945.*

Acknowledgements

Recalling the events and experiences of my time with No 249 Squadron in the Balkan Air Force has been made possible though the encouragement, support and assistance of members of my family, my friends, ex-POWs and ex-249ers.

    To Peg, my wife and my children; Ann for using her personal correspondence; Caroline for her able technology, Sir John Grandy and other fellow air and ground crews of the Squadron, Brian Cull for information from *249 at War,* Ray Stebbings, a fellow POW who also survived for including his cartoons; all those many others whose passing help I may have overlooked – Thank you for all you have done.

Foreword

By Marshal of the Royal Air Force **Sir John Grandy** GCB, GCVO, KBE, DSO, *first Officer Commanding No.249 Squadron in World War II, later Chief of the Air Staff, on retirement appointed by Her Majesty to be Constable at Windsor Castle.*

It was my historical privilege to reform No. 249 Squadron in May 1940 in preparation for the oncoming air battle known as the Battle of Britain. The Squadron served throughout that period in its history with great distinction, winning among other honours, the only Victoria Cross awarded to Fighter Command in WWII. It went on to gain many other battle honours in the epic air defence of Malta and in air operations as part of the Balkan Air Force.

Each stage of these historically famous air fighting periods of the war has been covered in successful publications. First in an overall, definitive history of the Squadron *249 at War* by Brian Cull, then *Gun Button the Fire* by Tom Neil, highlighting personal experiences through the Battle of Britain. The fight for survival of Malta with *Malta - The Thorn In Rommel's Side* was by the celebrated Laddie Lucas. Now Mac McCaig, who came to the fight from the distant Fiji Islands in the then – to us – remote Pacific Ocean, straddling the 180th meridian, has filled in the final WWII chapter of the Squadron's history.

Like so many of his Dominion and Colonial compatriots, McCaig found news about the heroic experiences of RAF fighter pilots during the Battle of Britain an irresistible call while in his final days at school in Fiji. He plunged into the exciting whirlwind of war while still a teenager. In his book, 'Fiji' (as he was called on the Squadron) takes us through his life with 249 in a compelling narrative about the Balkan Air Force phase. His life in the air over inhospitable terrain is a conscious struggle to kill or be killed, first in Spitfire Vs and then over a wider pattern of operations in Mustangs. Rapidly, as he says, losing the expendable nine lives that only a cat can claim.

He was shot down and baled out into the Greek mountains. He escaped capture and managed to rejoin his squadron. However his air warfare flying days came to an end when he was shot down a second time into a freezing Adriatic Sea. Failing to get the expected answer to his 'May-Day' calls he was captured by the SS and transported up into Germany. It is the beginning of a further struggle to survive between life and death, at times more brutal than air operations flying in the relative warmth of a fighter cockpit.

His strong Christian faith and firm belief in the power of good over evil stood Fiji in good stead and sustained him through the darkest times of his captivity.

John Grandy
March 2000

249 Squadron Mustangs in action over the Balkans – 1943

249 Squadron in the Balkans

No 249 Squadron gained a first place of honour through the names of its many famous and other lesser-known fighter pilots during World War II. In answer to a question by 'Laddie' Lucas (MP) in 1953, in the House of Commons, 249 was identified as being "one of the top scoring fighter squadrons (in numbers of enemy aircraft destroyed) during the Second World War." The Under Secretary of State for Air said no official records were prepared as to the claims made by individual fighter squadrons. However it is generally held that No. 249 did gain the distinction of top scoring fighter squadron with 349 enemy aircraft destroyed, 117 probables and 252 damaged. To this outstanding record 249's pilots added further claims of 137 locomotives destroyed, 187 probably destroyed or damaged, 135 railway wagons destroyed and 1,091 damaged, 663 MT vehicles destroyed and 1,079 damaged.

It was this overall wartime achievement that gained the following decorations during service with the Squadron: the only VC awarded to Fighter Command in WW2; 3 DSOs; 37 DFCs plus 6 Bars; 7 DFMs plus 2 Bars.

No 249 Squadron was formed in August 1918 from an amalgamation of Nos 400 and 450 Flights, flying Short 184 seaplanes and with access to Felixstowe F2As, Curtiss H12s and 16 flying boats at Killingholme. It was disbanded on 8th October 1919.

Under Squadron Leader Grandy (now Marshal of the Royal Air Force, Sir John) it was reformed on 16th May 1940 at Church Fenton and fought with great distinction through the Battle of Britain in Hurricanes and Spitfires. Many names emerged with honour from the air battles and will live on: Barton, Barclay, Davies, Neil,

Thompson, Beazeley, Veils, Nicolson, Kellet, to identify but a few of the 'Few'.

James Nicolson's Victoria Cross is displayed in the Battle of Britain Museum of the Royal Air Force Museum, Hendon. Hit by three cannon shells from a Messerschmidt 110, severely wounded and with his Hurricane cockpit in flames he was about to bale out when he noticed the attacking ME110 overshooting him. He delayed abandoning his crippled Hurricane and although in extreme pain regained his cockpit and shot the 110 down before baling out. His was an act of supreme bravery, outstanding even among so many examples of great courage shown by 249's pilots.

The Squadron was adopted by the people of the Gold Coast (Ghana) in November 1940. In Malta from May 1941, under the command of Squadron Leader 'Butch' Barton, the Squadron added fresh lustre to its name in the air defence of the island, first with Hurricanes and then with Spitfires. Fighting against enemy aircraft odds of sometimes 10 and 20 to 1 and facing fatigue, poor rations and inadequate equipment 249 (with other R.A.F. fighter squadrons) triumphed through 841 tons of bombs that pounded their main airfield at Takali.

More famous names emerged from this stage of the conflict: Turner, Grant, "Laddie" Lucas (see *Malta – The Thorn in Rommel's Side* published by Stanley Paul), McNair, "Screwball" Buerling, Hesslyn, Daddo-Langlois, Palliser, Plagis, te Kloot, Woods, Brennan, Hash, MacQueen, Mitchell, Rae, Lee, Jones, Seed, Kennedy. Under Squadron Leader Lynch (C.O. at that time) the squadron destroyed the 1,000th enemy aircraft claimed by the Malta air defences.

These were just some of the heroic pilots who came from Britain and from all over the Commonwealth; there were many others. Furthermore, the devoted tenacity of the groundcrews at this harassing time can never be forgotten; they made the air victories possible.

In Italy from 1943 to the end of World War Two, 249 Squadron operated across the Adriatic Sea from Italy as part of the Balkan Air Force. First under Colvin and then te Kloot and finally Edmondson.

The Squadron played a vital role in harassing the Germans with relentless dive-bombing and strafing missions. During this period its pilots added to the Squadron's notable score of successes, destroying aircraft whenever they could be found and taking a heavy toll of locomotives, railway rolling stock, motor transport and enemy troops.

When the Spitfire Vcs were replaced with Mustang IIIs, 249 ranged deep into Northern Greece, Yugoslavia and Austria. For a time, a flight of 249 aircraft was based on a grass strip north of Trikkila (Greece). From there it attacked targets as far afield as Bulgaria, thus giving rise to its claim of being the only RAF fighter squadron in WW2 to operate behind enemy lines in Europe.

The Squadron moved to Prkos in Yugoslavia in 1945 flying Spitfire IXs, until it was re-equipped with new Mustang IVs in Brindisi. It was disbanded on 16th August 1945 while under the temporary and final WW2 command of Flt/Lt. Ashworth.

No 249 Squadron, Officers Commanding – World War II

Sqn/Ldr	J. Grandy	May 1940 – December 1940
Sqn/Ldr	R.A. Barton	December 1940 – July 1941
Flt/Lt	T.F. Neil	August 1941
Sqn/Ldr	R.A. Barton	August 1941 – December 1941
Sqn/Ldr	E.B. Mortimer-Rose	December 1941
Sqn/Ldr	H.J.S. Beazley	December 1941 – February 1942
Sqn/Ldr	P.S. Turner	February 1942 – March 1942
Sqn/Ldr	S.B. Grant	March 1942 – June 1942
Sqn/Ldr	P.B. Lucas	June 1942 – July 1942
Sqn/Ldr	R.A. Mitchell	July 1942 – August 1942
Sqn/Ldr	E.N. Woods	August 1942 – December 1942
Sqn/Ldr	M.G. McLeod	January 1943 – March 1943
Sqn/Ldr	J.J. Lynch	March 1943 – July 1943
Sqn/Ldr	E.N. Woods	July 1943 – December 1943
Sqn/Ldr	D.S, Colvin	December 1943 – May 1944
Sqn/Ldr	J. te Kloot	June 1944 – November 1944
Sqn/Ldr	C. Edmondson	December 1944 – June 1945
Flt/Lt	T.H.E.B. Ashworth	June 1945 – August 1945

During the last stages of the WW2 conflict the courage and morale of 249 Squadron's pilots, backed by magnificent ground support, sustained the Squadron through heavy losses from accurate German flak while adding to the unit's outstanding record. Colvin, te Kloot, Edmondson, Finlay, Beatson, McBain, Sinclair, Whittingham, Simmons, Davison, Manning, Ashworth, Younis, Muir, Briggs, Nichols and Monkman increased the Squadron's final tally of wartime decorations.

No. 249 Squadron was reformed in October 1945 at Eastleigh, Nairobi, Kenya, when No. 500 (County of Kent) was renumbered No. 249. There followed a sequence of moves and changes in aircraft types, from Baltimore IVs to Mosquito FB26s in Nairobi in 1945/46, Tempest F6s in Habbanlya, as part of the Middle East Fighter Force, Palestine in 1948, the Canal Zone, Vampire FBVs in 1950, Shaibah in 1951, Vampire FB IXs in Nairobi, Amman in 1954, Venom

Squadron Leader te Kloot, 249 Squadron, Balkan Air Force, 1944.

FB1s, Venom FB IVs in 1955, Cyprus in 1956, and Canal Zone operations, Sultanate of Muscat and Oman in 1957 and finally, Canberras in Akrotiri, Cyprus in 1957.

The Squadron was presented with its standard on 7th October 1966 by Air Chief Marshal (now M.R.A.F.) Sir John Grandy.

No. 249 (Gold Coast) Squadron was disbanded at Akrotiri, Cyprus on 24th February 1969 with the following message from the Air Officer Commanding in Chief Middle East Air Forces:

"Today marks -the end of an era with the disbandment of your illustrious squadron. It is very sad to me, with such a long association with the Middle/Near East area of operations, the running elephant will no longer be seen in Mediterranean skies. The long and distinguished history of 249 is one of which I know you can all be justly proud and I share that pride... In saying goodbye I would like to express the fervent hope that the famous No 249 will be resurrected at some time in the future so that once more it may take its rightful place alongside other first class squadrons of the Royal Air Force. Please give my warmest good wishes to all your officers and airmen and their families and congratulate them on a job very well done."

Pugnis Et Calcibus (With Fists And Heels)

CHAPTER 1

Into Action

The sun stabbed at us out of a sparkling blue sky. The drive was long, hot and very dusty, a real endurance of sweat, boredom and hope. We crossed dreary hours of burnt grass countryside, perched on the hard bum-numbing front seats of the squadron 15-cwt utility truck.

I'd quickly run out of small talk and the airman driver kept his exchanges to within what he judged to be the proper limits of officer/airman relationships. He couldn't know I was burning with curiosity, wanting so much to ask "What's it like?" Somehow I couldn't bring myself to break that artificial barrier with the real question on my mind: "What kind of a squadron is it?" I couldn't voice my anxieties by saying "What's the C.O. like? The pilots? The life they lead? Wherever it was he was taking me…

We ground on relentlessly in the sun. He was probably conscious of the big difference between us – wartime familiarities or no – yet here we were, together in isolation from the rest of the world, driving through an Italian summer afternoon in July. I was the new guy he had been ordered to collect from the Personnel Dispatch Centre in Naples. I was sure he would be giving his buddies the run-down on the new guy he'd picked up when the day was through. I was one of the officer pilot replacements and as God knew there were more than a few flying out on operations and not coming home again.

My empty, heat mesmerised, thoughts drifted on through the drone of the engine, the gear changes, when he crashed through them and the jolting of a poorly sprung chassis. My khaki shirt stuck wherever it touched in cooling sweat, the dust lines edging a pattern of orange brown across my face. I was indeed a stranger in a strange land and I was on my own.

I had left my very close wartime companion of many years back in the stinking austerity of Naples. He was one of those real solid chaps. We were closer than brothers for all the years we had worn uniforms. It was from way back. Leaving our peaceful homes in the distant islands of the Fiji Group, together we had endured the long, dull journey to Sydney, Australia, the weeks of boredom in a Transit Camp waiting for our onward ship to the war. More endless weeks of boredom on the tramp steamer across the Indian Ocean, dipping down into the Antarctic to avoid submarines and then the long hot train journey up from Durban to Rhodesia. We had sneaked and squeaked our way through the exciting stages of flying training and sewed on our wings as fighter pilots. Next stop 'Blighty' and the war; our dream of making it into The Royal Air Force was complete, we were almost there. Fiji was now just a vaguely distant memory; we remembered how we had listened anxiously to the overseas service of the BBC with its frightening bulletins of defeat in France. We had wanted only to get there and join the war before it all ended; an idea long since gone.

The first Fiji contingent in the RAF, 1943.

There were bumbles and bungles to put up with, but that exhilarating first flight in a Hurricane fighter swept aside our first disappointments; but on finishing Hurricane Operational Training fate seemed to have forgotten us. There was no front line fighter squadron for us to join. The time and the place were wrong and our hopes were dashed in a surplus of trained fighter pilots. We were side-tracked to staff pilot jobs on bleak, windswept Walney island, Barrow-in-Furness, a soulless, austere station training air gunners for Bomber Command. It had all but broken our spirits. We fought 'the powers that be' for over a year until a posting came through; for immediate replacements in the Middle East Air Force. Then, as if to exact some kind of price for it, the cold-blooded certainty of our joining the war separated our friendship with postings to different fighter squadrons. The parting had been a cruel, painful blow. We had stood, clasped hands, said little, then gone our separate ways to whatever was to come in the real killing war. Maybe I would never see him again…

Vague thoughts wandered around my mind in the dozy heat and the jolting of the truck. I felt uncertain, nothing to fasten onto, no sensation, nothing familiar to grasp. I floated in a dreamy kind of vacuum, not trying to arrest my mental wandering, merely to adjust to things in my new predicament. Yet I knew that every event and every moment over the past couple of years had been leading up to wherever this bouncing 15cwt, dust covered, truck was taking me. This was the be-all – even perhaps the end-all – of my time away from the peaceful normality of my home life in the Pacific islands. I was about to face the big challenge and I had no way of knowing how I would do with it, or – more importantly – what it would do with me. I wondered whether the difficulties I had experienced in striving to reach a front-line fighter squadron had somehow magnified its importance out of all proportion. How was it that a machine, an impersonal machine of war, could lure a schoolboy from the remote security of a place beyond the knowledge of most of the outside world? Fiji in the 1930s was still an almost unknown group of islands; aeroplanes were never seen in those tropical skies and boats carrying tourists and merchandise came only infrequently. How much things had changed for me since then.

We came to a junction my driver knew.

"This is it!" he said, sounding pleased to be at the journey's end. We bounced off the main road onto an even dustier unmade track, leaving billowing clouds of fine white dirt in our wake. Eventually, we arrived at a pattern of brown tents in rough lines; it was the squadron domestic site sitting alone atop an arid plateau. The drab brown lines of canvas were set in a treeless landscape with a distant view of the bright blue Adriatic Sea beyond. It was less than tidy, less than inspiring, but it was the home of my first front-line fighter squadron.

There was not a single aircraft in sight across the wide horizon or in the airspace overhead. We eased down through the outside line of tents. I sensed the driver was waiting for my instructions when he stopped at a large untidy mass of drooping canvas, its guy ropes, sagging noticeably.

"This is the Officers Mess, Sir," he said and I noticed a small sign stuck askew into the ground bearing that name. 'You could have fooled me!' I thought, as I stiff-leggedly dismounted, brushing the dust from my sweat-stained bush shirt.

"Thanks driver, for the ride," was all it needed. He went to the rear of the truck, lowered the tailboard, set down my camp kit-roll, a suitcase and my kit bag and drove off, leaving me standing there, uncertain of what to do next.

The Officers Mess Tent

An untidy-looking chap, Australian slouch-hat askew, deliberate in movement, friendliness written all over him, emerged from a smaller, isolated tent behind the Mess and spoke.

"G'day!" His voice had a quiet sound of authority, the nasal twang familiar to my colonial ears. "I'm the C.O. How are you? Have a good ride getting here?"

I felt better, right off. Something about him seemed to embrace me, not saying much but enough to know I'd found the place I wanted to be. If this was my war unit and this man the leader of it, I'd go with him into the fight. He looked like an outback sheep farmer exuding a warm confidence and comradeship.

"Good to meet you, Sir! It is a bloody awful drive but I'm pleased to be here at last! He must know it from my smile and the firm contact of our handshake. We exchanged names a little awkwardly.

"Right," he said "We've fixed a space for you, sharing with one other. That's how it is here, officers, two to a tent. Maybe I shouldn't put it this way but you'll be nearer the Mess than usual – you'll be taking the space of one of our South Africans; he went missing over Yugoslavia yesterday..." I couldn't find an answer to that. Lifting my stuff with his help we walked the few yards to the tent he indicated.

"I'll see you later in the Mess. We eat at 1830. Come and have a drink – if we've got any of the beer ration left – meet some of your fellow pilots."

He left me still uncertain but no longer alone.

Unfolding the camp bed I made it up – more for want of something to do than of necessity. I erected the struts for my canvas washbasin and placed it outside the tent flap. What next, I wondered. It wasn't what I'd expected. Three chaps came out and called their warm greetings with names of introduction. They were fellow fighter pilots. They offered help and information about the set up and seemed completely relaxed. I listened eagerly, not wanting to reveal my own innocence, but wanting to hear all about it. 'But about what?' I wondered, not knowing anything. It was going to take a lot before I exposed my personality to them; first I'd have to make my assessment of them all. Meeting new faces, making friendly greetings was only the first step, but a lot had to follow before I worked out and measured their characters. I was not a new pilot. I had more airborne experience than most of them, but they had the lead in operational flying and its attendant hazards. We'd find a way to communicate because we shared a common cause, a trained commitment to fight in the air, and perhaps to die doing it. There may be barriers between us, however, depending on the personalities that lay behind the masks.

Fighter pilot flying was essentially a loner performance; once in the cockpit and in the sky, all the decisions were yours – certainly you needed the support of other pilots within your formation, the ground crew who made it possible to get up there anyway, the administration behind all that and many other things – but in the end there was nobody sitting up there with you to tell you what to do and how to do it. There was only you.

Over the coming weeks I met the others in different places and at different times; some spontaneously warm and receptive, others more reserved, holding back, needing time to make a more studied judgement before accepting me. There were funny chaps and friendly or serious ones – and a great range of personalities in between. I wanted to hide my uncertainty; not show my shyness. They were more than my fellow pilots and the ground crew who had seen it all. They were my superiors. Not in rank on the ground but as fighters well versed in the brash realities of a killing war. The pilots had more experience in doing what I had come here to do; most of them were old hands at survival. I felt I had yet to be initiated to their standards and to be accepted as a reliable addition to their team.

I knew over the time to come I would share tensions, the aggression of operational sorties, the fears from flak when it burst all around you seeming somehow so harmless yet lethal and the ultimate fear of being shot down.

'The real test' they told me with quiet conviction was in 'killing without being killed'.

The Squadrons losses were all about the heavy and accurate flak the Germans on the other side of the Adriatic had assembled. "You will be extremely lucky to see any Luftwaffe at all, but you can be sure when you are over their territory they'll be ranging in on you – whether you hear the sound of a radar lock-on or not."

As a Squadron we lived an austere and comfortless existence apart from the rest of the Air Force. The hardships and the denial of any personal pleasures were a real part of our lives. But they somehow fashioned us into a companionable gathering of men with a common cause. The airmen, NCOs and the Officers were all segregated in tent lines, bogs and messes but the food – if that's what they called it – and the water bowser with its rationed supplies were 'one for all and all for one'. I recall one day asking for the CO's whereabouts and an airman pointing up the slope and saying "That's him sitting on the throne up there..." Sure enough, there he was, his slouch hat unmistakable as he squatted on the crude wooden bench with a hole in the middle and bucket beneath sheltered on three sides only from the wind and dust!

There were happy times when the mail came in at irregular intervals or when a group of airmen came over to challenge us at volleyball or someone shouted across the site saying that the truck was going down to the beach for a swim. Out of the day-to-day activities and despite the mixture of men from many places and with many differences, a mutually supporting family of some one hundred souls emerged without anyone spelling it out like that. However, there was no place for emotions; we all held back on feelings. Getting too close to anybody in friendship was a bad idea – chaps were disappearing all the time. There were occasions of conflict but never too extreme. We may not always have liked one another but we knew that until we died, were shot down or lived out our full tour of duty we must fly and fight together.

CHAPTER 2

First Blood

My blooding in the killing war came after they'd checked me out with a few training flights on their Spit Vcs, dive bombing with practice smoke bombs and some free flying to get the feel of it. I had a sense of uncertainty. I knew so little but I yearned to 'have a real go'.

Five of us were briefed for a dawn dive-bombing attack and strafing mission on a reported German fuel and explosive ammunition dump in one of those deep valleys with mountains sheer on either side. We would have time over target of fifteen minutes to find something to shoot at and could expect to encounter a lot of flak. The Germans never exposed things without mighty protection everywhere. They knew how to do it and they knew how to do it well.

I dressed in the dark, feeling the shock of cold water dipped from the canvas bucket positioned outside my tent. The other chap sharing with me stirred and called a sleepy message "Good luck, Fiji!" At pre-dawn breakfast I looked at the plate of greasy soya bean sausage and hard egg dipped from a float of bubbling fat and inwardly heaved. It was not for me; my stomach refused anything at all, it was tight as a drum, half through excitement, half through fear. Who knew what was to come of it? Scrambling into the back of the cheerless, cold 15cwt we jolted out of the sleeping campsite down the hill to the flying strip. There was no talk.

'Spy' was there before us in his briefing tent ready with his charts marked to show the target and flak positions. The truth is, he hadn't a bloody clue! Those flak positions could be weeks out of date after coming through the Partisan network via goodness knows how many channels and being corrupted at each stop. We all listened to him with stretched nerves wanting to know what he had to say, but not knowing whether it had any real meaning.

"Your target is said to have a fair old cover of flak in the surrounding hills, mostly forty mill, but you can expect some lighter stuff lower down, twenty mill and machine gun. The set up is for a very high speed one-off pass with the sun behind you in the dive. If you hit this one, it will make Guy Fawkes night look like a dwindling candle in a fresh breeze…"

He stopped when his funny little joke failed to raise a chortle. I lifted an eye to the weak yellow light from a solitary naked bulb hanging on the central tent pole. It sparkled a reflection in his steel rimmed glasses. He was a real good guy, a former schoolteacher, spelling out the routine ritual. We all knew his humour. He was very much on our side and deep down a real softy. He went on, "I think all hell could erupt from contagious explosions. I suggest you watch your pull out after going below mountain top height, it'll still be darkish down there. Lets hope they are all still asleep…" Another pause to smile invitingly. Dear old Spy, what did he know about pull-out heights in the valleys across the water!

Our section leader took over, an old hand Flight Sergeant pilot. We stood listening in silence while he added his bit about the flight route, the spacing between aircraft after reaching height, watching every corner of the sky around us, radio silence and attack formation over the target area. Spy added a few words about escape and evasion if anyone was hit and had to bale out. Who wanted to think of that! Their words tightened in my gut. I couldn't stand the suspense, I just wanted to move out to the flight line and my allocated Spit. I glanced at my flight map for the hundredth time and saw again the circle I'd drawn on it with a cross for the target.

Once strapped in and started up my tension eased. Our Spits, with bombs slung like clumsy appendages clinging to the underbelly clips, roared away down the pierced steel planking strip in pairs, climbing out into the gaining light of dawn in complete radio silence.

The bright sun coloured the eastern skyline away to starboard brilliant shades of orange and red. I moved my thrumming aircraft out into battle formation, one pair line abreast as briefed and three

(Left) The Author, about to set off for his first 'op' in a Spitfire Mk.V.

(Below) One of 249's Mustangs after an emergency landing – undercart shot away.

Arming a Spitfire for dive-bombing activities.

up sun and slightly behind us. Ear cocked I listened closely to the steady vibration of the big Merlin up front, tight in concentration, checking the instruments, keeping station, sweeping the sky, seeing the deep purple of sea below gradually lighten as the rising sun lifted the gloom. We gained height, steady on course, watching for the hostile shoreline to come out of the morning haze. It looked massively threatening in its grandeur, a wondrous sight. The huge ranges of semi-black mountains seemed formidable. Slowly, as the light increased they revealed a stark beauty and an unspoken warning of the perils of going down, baling out. As we crossed the coastline everything seemed quiet below us.

Suspended high in the sharp clear air we manoeuvred into position to launch our formation into destructive action. The target area was a quiet Lilliputian pattern just visible through the thin mist lifted by the first shafts of the rising sun. The protective shadows of darkness were melting away.

I checked circuit switches ON, gun button to all guns FIRE and carefully flicked through the pre-attack drill. The leader's voice crackled into my startled headphones, breaking the long-held radio silence.

"Ernie Red – target below us now – eight o'clock – at the river bend road Junction – bomb as briefed – climb out into sun."

His terse message hung in the air while I waited, screwed up, tight as a drum – "Going in NOW!"

I watched the silhouette of his Spitfire roll and swoop vertically towards the ground between the mountains which towered on either side. I followed him, searching for the target zone, head down, eyes staring through the windscreen, watching in absolute concentration, occasionally glancing at the instruments, following the image of his Spit below me against the fast approaching ground beneath us. I tried to focus on all the things I must do: trim the plane, watch the altimeter unwind, keep what was happening down there in full view. I had no time to think, everything was instinct, it all had to be done in a bewildering flash of seconds. His plane whipped through my line of vision, flattening out into level flight, vortices of condensation streaming back from his wing tips. Then he was pulling away, the two bombs small and just visible as they left his aircraft. Two lurid spurts of orange flame erupted quicker than I expected and interrupted my concentration for a moment. In that same instant I saw the target shapes, two camouflaged haystacks, well hidden, below me and slightly ahead. Quickly centring my gunsight I pressed the firing button. The plane juddered in recoil as the deadly cannon shells spewed out, drumming their message of destruction. The altimeter showed me critically low. At that speed I needed a lot of space to round out of the dive without completely blacking out as the blood drained away from my brain through the imposed excess in G-force. I eased hard back on the stick fighting the blackout, counting one – two – three – RELEASE. The Spit bucked slightly under me as my two deadly projectiles launched for the target. I pulled harder on the stick, banking to starboard as I climbed upwards at full throttle into the glowing brightness of the rising sun. I was still in one piece. A quick scan upwards and there was the reassuring sight of my leader. Up I went, wondering what had happened in the time between rolling into the dive to gaining height again, which had disappeared from my conscious mind.

Looking down I saw below a hellhole of fire and smoke rising through the mist, spewing upwards like a volcano. As each plane thundered in, the carnage increased. A sight of awful destruction. The dumps exploded with a violence and colour I'd never seen.

Suddenly my Spit bucked in the climb. A confetti of murderous black puffs framed the aircraft, seeming to fill my part of the valley, exploding violently into every space around me. Surely it wasn't possible to climb through a barrage such as this and not be hit? I was scared, recalling the pre-flight briefing from Spy and our section leader... "If you can see the bloody stuff exploding all around you, that's OK. You'll never see the one that really counts…"

One by one they all came up out of it and we climbed out of 40mm range, joining again into battle formation and heading along the coastline, slightly inland. I had lived a whole lifetime in that attack, but I had made it and I felt good – thank God! I longed to go back and take a look at the target and review our handiwork, but that, of course, would be suicide. Something of the havoc was visible: black smoke rising straight up into the still air between the mountains and flashes of colour as one huge explosion down there bred another.

I relaxed a little, feeling good that I had come through something extraordinary and was still alive. The plane felt OK, the sound of engine and instrument readings reassuring. I slid my bomb-lightened plane across the tail of Ernie Red Leader and moved closer in to give him the 'thumbs up'. His aircraft seemed OK as well. I positioned again up sun, disregarding the few black puffs still bursting impotently below us.

His voice came again, calm and reassuring, a human connection between the five of us each in his solitary cockpit still pumping adrenaline like crazy.

"Ernie Red – we'll search the valley road at three o'clock before heading back to base."

He was taking a chance. We hadn't been briefed on this one. It sounded like a bonus for doing the main target well. I felt the excitement within me rise again – sweet exhilaration. Another voice followed, almost superimposed and crackling with obvious excitement as his message came out

"Ernie Red Three – there's a car on the road – four o'clock – moving north – a big dust cloud behind."

Quick as a flash the leader responded, declaring his intention. He'd seen it and he was not going to miss this one.

"Red One, I'll take it – going down – Two follow me – Three, Four, Five stay for cover."

I rolled to starboard with him, losing height fast, searching eagerly for the sight they had reported. Then lovely, lovely, there it was, stark naked, a tidy, well camouflaged shape clearly outlined in the hazy light, sitting stationery in the middle of a lonely road. It looked like a staff car. They'd surely seen and heard us; or were they hoping against it, waiting, uncertain for a desperate second or two.

I checked the gun button to FIRE, seeing streamer puffs of tracer shells flashing from the Leader's Spit, waiting precious seconds before he moved out of my line of fire. He zoomed away and I fixed my own gunsight with tight concentration at the centre line of the car. I pressed the button all the way in and the guns responded in recoil as I strafed for the kill. It was hypnotic. I remembered almost too late to pull out. In my last flashing vision I spotted three figures running wildly for cover like desperate ants, frantically trying to escape almost certain death. I'd seen the leader's cannon shells and bullets splash and kick all around them. Had I fired too soon, out of range, my fire pattern to wide to hit anything?

The scene vanished below me before my own strikes showed. By the grace of God I missed the crest of the hill by a matter of a few feet. It was pulse racing stuff, my whole being at extreme pitch, climbing wide to reform on the leader as we turned for the coastline. I heard one of the voices transmit from above.

"You got it! You got the bastard! Good shooting, he's a flamer!"

249 Squadron 1944 – The Spitfire Era

FIJI TO BALKAN SKIES · 29

It startled me. I screwed round in my seat harness, stretching to see what he was talking about. The car was disappearing in a cloud of smoke and devouring flame. It was my kill. What a beaut!

"Reform Ernie Red – returning to base." Climbing again for height we headed out over the safety of the sea for home again.

I checked the fuel gauges and adjusted the pitch control for easy cruising speed, letting go a huge sigh of relief, venting off something from my over-stimulated system. My initiation had involved excitement to the very fullest – it had been bloody marvellous! Better still, we were safe again… at least for now.

My home from home, 1944.

CHAPTER 3

The Killing War

Our closely confined existence settled into an acceptable routine of living. Each day had its parts and looking for my place within them was neither difficult nor demanding. It was a kind of mixture between the quiet boredom of camp life with little more to do than reflect or meet the minor duties imposed on an officer. The flying sorties came at irregular intervals with the occasional training flight or the pre-briefed operations, as the call demanded.

The pilots, Senior Non-Commissioned and Commissioned Officers, lived separated lives on the ground but once in the air it was all about experience and rank differences disappeared. Somehow it all worked. The peculiar logic imposed by tradition throughout the Royal Air Force was an accepted way of life for us. Our tent lines and our Mess tents were sited apart on the ground but in the air our competence, our fears and our emotions were the same. It was all held in check by drill and the discipline we'd known from the very first day in the RAF; lightly imposed and loyally followed. We did as we were told, following the way it was ordered, meticulously and to the best of our ability knowing that finally, success or failure was in the hands of each individual and the lap of the gods. We had a certain confidence in the system. It was correct and we knew that; a tried and tested way of life. There was no comfort of any kind. The tents were nothing more than a shelter in which to sleep and eat. Even our daily shit lacked overhead protection in those first days of camp life. Keeping what clothes we had marginally clean and dry required ingenuity. The central pole holding the tents above us offered the only concession to vanity – a small mirror. Yet it was essential we maintained a standard between and through the rank differences. The small canvas bucket outside my tent had its precise place alongside my washbasin standing neatly on its tripod. What could we have done without canvas!

Sluicing in cold water each morning was a bracing experience. Freezing in the winter months, scooping off the thin film of dust in the summer, careful to preserve and not waste the daily ration from our centrally positioned water tank.

There was something of a social event in the daily visit to the 'thrones' allocated to each rank level of squadron personal. Their elevated position saved many of us a wasted walk. You could check for a vacant position before setting out to trudge up there. One of our comics dropped the comment "I hope the Ities who empty the buckets each night are careful not to mix the officers with the airmen's shit!" Why it was ever reasoned that we needed separate places with identical centre holed pinewood boards according to rank – officers, NCOs and airmen – failed the test of real logic. These rules and regulations where devised by unknown others in distant places. We all shared the same rain when sitting there in the wet, the same heat in the baking sun… but we were not allowed to share the same squat holes!

During warm summer days the red dust was the bane of our restricted lives. It penetrated everywhere, into everything, clothes, beds, and hair, all over our bodies. Any exertion produced sweat, to which the dust stuck immediately. We were rationed to two visits to the remotely sited showers each week although in summer the blessed sea was fortunately within reach.

Our lives were focused on one thing – aeroplanes – what we were ordered to do in them, what they were capable of, when they had to do it and the weather conditions that controlled everything. We knew that our orders started somewhere unknown and far away. A stream of information about what was going on across the Adriatic Sea trickled mysteriously into our centres of intelligence where it was studied, analysed and used to fashion an operational plan designed to inflict as much damage as we could to the enemy.

Decisions were made and operations devised for us to attempt to execute and survive – destructive dive bombing raids, searching out and strafing anything mechanical that moved along the desolate roads or railway lines. Finding anything of the Luftwaffe in the Balkan skies or on the ground was always our dream, but mostly a hopeless one.

I had little of the real killer instinct, never wanting more than to successfully hit the targets, inflicting destruction without having to witness the death or pain my bombs and bullets might have inflicted on other human beings. These horrors and agonies were something I left at each target area without further thought, turning for home, relieved only that I had survived another sortie. My self-preservation instinct prevailed above every other feeling. Occasionally when debriefing after an operation Spy passed on information about the damage we had inflicted in some detail. His telling of it was but history by the time it reached us.

We were no more callous in our attitude towards the enemy than we were concerning our own pilots who failed to come back; we simply could not afford to become emotional about it. I knew I never wanted to see the killings, never wanted to make claims about the human bodies destroyed. The ammunition dumps, bridges, motor transport targets, whether empty or full of soldiers, locomotives, railway trucks – they were all something legitimate for complete destruction. They were just 'the enemy' with never a thought about any human element within them. I knew only to go out and to come back intact. Those whose place it was to order us into action, who lived remote from the danger of flak guns always instructed that we should strike hard without endangering our planes, as they were 'our most valuable asset in the war effort'.

"Yes, and so am I!" I would think to myself.

We had daily reminders that the enemy across the water, though almost beaten, could still strike us down. Our war-weary Spitfire Vcs did not always return in the same numbers that took off. 'Vacant' tent spaces occurred regularly and a brutal system, a kind of musical chairs of life and death, dictated that we could occupy a vacant space and attempt to improve our own position with regards to our proximity to the Mess tent, shortening the walk in the rain, the cold or the winter snow. In addition, the custom was that upon a pilot's death or disappearance any useful trophies of war, guns acquired illicitly or special non-uniform jackets etc could be shared out by close friends. Personal items, regardless of whether they might be sidetracked or lost in transit must always be sent home to the next of kin. Regulations required that each item be listed, witnessed and packaged for shipment into an ever-busy pipeline destined for a saddened addressee in some far off place. An official signal always preceded the despatching of personnel effects. There were only two kinds of message: one contained an element of hope, informing the recipient that the pilot had been seen to bale out and was believed to be 'safe'; the second said that he was believed to have been killed.

Our fight against the unseen enemy took us over the rugged and mountainous terrain in Yugoslavia, Albania and Greece. Balkan country, where roads were few and far between, railway lines rarer still. It was favourable guerrilla warfare country. Horses, mules and foot soldiers could often outmanoeuvre modern mechanised vehicles of war. Nevertheless, the fighting peasants needed our help. Anything that moved, either MT convoys or trains towing a line of trucks were fair game. Sometimes we sought out specific targets, dive-bombing and strafing military convoys or concentrations, the bridges they must cross or the roads they must use. Armed reconnaissance sweeps followed. The German flak was highly organised and deadly when it found our vulnerable aircraft.

The summaries of our frequent raids across the water were written in very matter of fact language. They gave no insight into to the adrenaline-pumping life-and death action they described.

> "Six aircraft each with two five hundred pound bombs, instant fuses, armed recce Podgorica to Metsevo. Bombed MT column between WIT270907 WB278978. Four direct hits – two near misses. Bombed between V1133790 to 135800. Two direct hits – two near misses. Intense light flak."

> "Six aircraft – armed rec. – each two five hundred pound bombs instant fuses, Brod to Sarajevo. Bombed locomotives at XK1817. Two bombs

falling on railway track exploding among wagons. Train strafed, locomotive destroyed. At XK3046 bombed railway sidings and buildings. Four bombs exploded on buildings; two near misses. At XM2085 locomotive and four coaches destroyed by strafing. Strafed locomotive and wagons at S00504, XM2095, XM3078, XM2085. Claims from strafing three locomotives destroyed, two damaged. Four passenger coaches damaged – about thirty wagons hit."

"Twelve aircraft – two five hundred pound bombs inst. fuse – armed recce coastal gun positions Lussinpiecolo. Twelve bombs exploded in target area – ammunition dump destroyed – eight bombs near misses – two overshot target – two fell on top of hill. Intense medium flak. Two aircraft hit but returned to base"

It was a deadly game. Each plane carried its pilot, human and vulnerable to the fear and apprehension that came with each armed sortie. Would the plane carrying them be reliable enough to get there, execute the task, and get them back across that wide stretch of Adriatic Sea? What if they had to bale out over the hostile Balkan terrain with its sparse population and the difficulty of rescue? What if they fell into the hands of the warring partisan factions, some of whom were against the allied cause. Suppose there was a sudden change in the weather conditions?

Most returned OK. Some did not. Some were shot down and killed; others reported missing; some disappeared without trace; others were taken prisoner by the Germans whilst a few escaped or evaded capture with the assistance of friendly partisans, to eventually return to their squadron. Sometimes there were miracles of survival and sometimes fatalities not directly attributable to enemy action. Occasionally attempts to find a pilot who had been shot down resulted in the loss of some of those engaged in the rescue operation either through enemy flak or misjudgement.

"A flight of four Spitfire Vcs strafed a line of lorries and a German staff car parked on the road. The leader warned about tall poplar trees lining the road. One aircraft pulled out late from his strafing run, hit a tree, tearing

off his starboard main plane, flipped over, exploded in a ball of fire killing the pilot. The vehicles in the convoy were destroyed."

"During one bombing sortie a pilot baled out hit by flak. Several attempts failed to locate him. The following day the search continued. By chance he was seen as three Luftwaffe Me 109s attacked the squadron Spitfires out of the sun. One was shot down and one Spitfire went down, the pilot baling out. The searchers returned to base short of fuel. The search recommenced, the first pilot was found and the second, both rescued by Walrus flying boat landing on the coastline."

"On another occasion the Spitfire was hit, the bullet passing through the pilot's flying suit sleeve, ricocheting off his armoured seat, through his other sleeve and out again. He was completely unharmed."

Several, of our 'disappearances' came to light later through the commission of enquiry appointment to discover what had happened to 'missing' pilots. One aircraft had been hit after strafing a locomotive with about 20 wagons. He'd made two passes; on the second, one of the wagons exploded in a sheet of red flame. He flew westwards, baled out at five thousand feet and was seen to land safely, stow his 'chute and make for some nearby woods. He waved to his two companions above and disappeared. The commission revealed that he had been captured by Bulgarian partisans, tortured and killed.

Here and there the stress of operations was relieved by an unintentional funny story – always embellished in the retelling and serving to remind us we were all still able to laugh at one another in the right kind of way. They were spontaneous flashes of fun that lifted some of the weight from our tense lives.

A new pilot, a highly strung lad with too few flying hours experience, was enjoying his first operational sortie in battle formation, line abreast, spread wide, eyes sweeping everywhere as he'd been briefed. Lagging behind the formation he was seeking to catch them up. Suddenly his voice broke the golden rule of R/T silence when on the way to a target.

"Hey Look, chaps, ducks! Five o'clock high."

The leader's voice responded instantly in full tones of reprimand. "Ducks? At twenty thousand feet? – You bloody fool!"

The chap never again confused feathered birds on the wing with heavy flak! He never again lagged behind in battle formation and he never lived the incident down – though he was always teased with good humour.

On another occasion one of our South African pilots baled out into the snow. Struggling through endless drifts, worried that he would freeze to death in the vastness of the desolate mountains, with not a sound to be heard, not another human in sight, he struggled on. His fast fading spirits revived when he came upon big footprints in the frightening isolation of wilderness. Eagerly he followed their general direction in the hope they'd lead him to rescue. His last reserves of energy almost gone, loud shouting from up the slope heralded the presence of partisans. He could not make out what they were talking about but was thankful when they led him

Mustang with flak damage – a near thing!

to their hideout. Once there, an interpreter sorted it out. All faces around him listened intently during the two-way conversation. The footprints that led him to safety were not made by human beings but some kind of wild animal. "They are always hungry in the winter snow!" he was told with a great deal of primitive laughter.

During that same intense winter the squadron flew in escort to six Dakota aircraft briefed to land at a secret airstrip in wooded and mountainous countryside. The partisans were encircled by the Germans and preparing to make a way through the closing ring. They were handicapped by a large number of wounded who would undoubtedly be killed by the enemy if left behind. Our sortie was briefed to bring them out The Dakotas flew three rescue flights with success. It was a mission of great mercy.

The enemy forces were gradually withdrawing northwards from Albania and Greece. This dictated considerable movement of trains and MT convoys. A welcome increase in targets for us.

The Author in the cockpit of a Mustang – 1944

Our Spitfire Vs were replaced by Mustangs – a lovely aircraft giving us a welcome increase in radius of action and greater firepower. It was a gentleman's cockpit after the austere and battle-worn Spits.

The very first sortie ranged across Bulgaria and out on to the Salonika plain in Greece. Four locomotives and an armoured car were damaged. An MT column was attacked and several 'flamers' claimed. The No.2 to the CO was hit, and baled out at twelve thousand feet.

The first Mustang lost. He was seen to land safely and make for cover. The Greek partisans found him. Forced to remain in their custody while awaiting rescue arrangements he endured a mistaken bombing raid by RAF Wellingtons and a machine gun attack from a rival partisan force. During his stay he was offered the exclusive 'attention' of a pretty young partisan woman, though later he claimed to have declined her services!

The Mustang's cooling radiator was slung in a wide aerodynamic scoop below the fuselage. It was the aircraft's 'Achilles heel' – requiring only a single bullet penetration to slowly leak away the vital glycol liquid coolant. One thin plume of white trailing smoke was the fatal signal for others within a formation. A pilot told he was 'trailing' knew it was but a matter of time before his engine overheated and seized up. The call came through to one courageous chap who finally rolled over and baled out. He had hardly touched the ground and collected his shocked wits when a group of peasant women rushed onto the scene. They ignored him and went straight for his parachute! Clothing material was desperately short in those parts. Chetnik soldiers arrived and took him to General Mihailovitchch's headquarters. There he found seventeen other American and English aircrew. They lived well enough while trying to persuade their captors to allow a rescue mission and return to Italy. The Chetniks allowed radioed messages to be passed back to Italy but nothing more. Mihailovitch was riding a political fence – on friendly terms with the German Commandant but wanting to hold on to a bargaining source for assistance from the allies for his fight against Tito's partisans. While waiting for some sort of rescue, our pilot watched a football match. He suddenly found and faced one of the Germans in full uniform. He saluted him aggressively. The response was a clicking of heels and 'Heil Hitler'

As the partisans gained the upper hand attacking the Chetniks the aircrew with them were forced to retreat. Food became extremely scarce and was finally reduced almost nothing. Our pilot realised it could all end in death through starvation. He escaped the column, finding the partisans some distance away. They identified his credentials, accepted him and arranged for his return to the squadron. He had lost three stone, suffered persistent diarrhoea, had tapeworms and was infested with lice around his balls, under his armpits and in his head. In recognition of his achievement and conduct during captivity he was awarded a Distinguished Flying Medal.

With the Mustangs longer range we could now hit anything in the Balkan area, concentrating on more aggressive reconnaissance, going out at first light of day, sweeping far and wide, seeking signs of movement of anything mechanical that strayed out of the darkness, especially trains. There was no sight more thrilling than a mortally struck locomotive exploding in a billowing cloud of erupting steam.

249 Squadron 1944 – After conversion to Mustangs

249 Squadron Mustangs and pilots.

Each fortnight the squadron detached four aircraft south to Brindisi to raid out across Albania, hunting across the Salonika plain where the enemy had been unmolested for overlong. Our lives in Brindisi were like being back in civilisation after the wilderness; a town once again with people, shops, (such as they were) roadways and buildings. The Mess we shared was a solid stone structure, a proper place for the human beings who occupied it. We had *beds* and a place to eat such as we'd known in previous times. The lavatories *flushed*, the showers were there for the asking! There was no luxury about the place but after the bareness of tents and the campsite back at the Squadron HQ we took a real liking to the change.

We soon adjusted to our new found comforts and while waiting for the signals for the next day's operations to come in we got stuck into whatever drink could be had. It oiled the mental process, softened our outlook, illuminated a hidden corner or two, and allowed a bit of relief from the intensity of our single-minded existence and moved the talk onto something different from attack systems, what our chances were of being hacked down.

Back at Squadron HQ a new acquisition had emerged. We had traded some of our much prized spirit ration for a hut! It was a real plus swapping the Mess tent for a firmer structure and we took pride in our new possession. Everyone had given something towards it. Everyone had helped with its final construction and internal set up. It was only of one skin corrugated iron but it had enough space for a bar made from overload tanks and packing cases in one corner, with a sitting section complete with a clever piece of innovation for a fire and a separate space for our dining table. It was one of those improvements that gave pleasure to all of us way beyond its material worth or style and with the coming winter months our life would be vastly improved. Of course nothing could eliminate the walk to our tents for sleeping on the canvas stretcher beds after the relative warmth of the hut. Ah well, we couldn't have it all ways!

Gradually the talk expanded and we moved into war experiences elsewhere, before the squadron and before the Mustangs and the welcome change of detachments at Brindisi.

One of the chaps began to tell a story about his brother Charlie, who had been a pilot in the Battle of Britain. From the start I was fascinated.

"My brother Charlie's 'Number Two' was called Charlie as well. They were close, very close, a kind of union of spirits. He told me he valued that chap's friendship more than he could put into words. They joined up together, trained together and were on a squadron together. They survived together. The war machine had not only processed them but in a strange kind of way it had forged their friendship. Before the war they were both young and full of fire but the RAF gave them a common purpose although they had both been nervous at first about whether they would make the grade as fighter pilots. It was a kind of wartime relationship neither of them tried to put into words – maybe they never understood it – it was just something between them in those days when so many pilots were being hacked down in great numbers. Both calling one another Charlie had sort of come out of the blue. It was a kind of joke between them, a sort of intimate code name. The chaps around must have noticed it but, like many things in those early days, it was just accepted. Chuckling, he paused, telling us his brother mentioned they'd said things like, 'Hey, Charlie! what about a few pints at the Spreadeagle?' Their mates on the squadron were even known to say, 'you two Charlies coming out for a break – a few pints?' Things like that. Accepting the special relationship, their silly common nickname. You know, my brother was a special kind of chap and maybe so was his friend Charlie. I don't know – he was always talking about him when he came home on leave, he said his friend Charlie had a kind of sixth sense – always seemed to make right decisions when it counted most."

I recognised something similar in the way I had developed a very firm friendship with a chap with that same nickname. I remembered how Charlie and I had both journeyed away from Fiji together, trained for our wings together, reached the UK together, passed through fighter operational training unit together, been side swiped into that appalling and wasteful year as stooge pilots in Training

Command, fought our way out of it together and posted overseas to the Middle East together. Then wallop, separated into two different squadrons without the slightest 'kiss-my-arse' or any other kind of preliminary! That was the way of it.

I wondered where his reminiscence was going. He was going on a bit, but I could see that he was deadly serious. He continued with his story.

His brother, Charlie, had told him about an incident that happened when he was leading a section of four Hurricanes scrambled to intercept a big enemy raid coming over the south east coast. Their intention was to pounce on the long stream of bombers from up sun.

"They were holding radio silence, knowing that if they spoke the enemy would pin-point them and their advantage would be lost. Charlie was just about to give the order to go in for the kill when an R/T warning crackled into his earphones, startling the bloody daylights out of him.

"Wait, Charlie! Wait!"

He recognised the voice as that of his Number Two who was out there high above on his starboard wing. It had an excited pitch to it, but he couldn't see why. He swept the sky around him for signs of danger. Then he saw the purpose of the warning. A squadron of Spits also scrambled to take on the raid were going down, diving for the front of the bomber stream. High above them, coming out of the blinding sun was a great gaggle of ME109s, swooping for a deadly attack from their height advantage. The call had come because Charlie Number Two had spotted the situation before anyone else. His "Wait, Charlie wait' had saved my brother's flight from almost certain extinction. His judgement and timing were perfect!

They let the 109s lose their height advantage, get below them, then BOOM down they went on them like a pack of wolves – and from high up sun. The Huns didn't know what had hit them!"

He showed some excitement as he told it, almost as if he'd been there with his brother. We waited in polite silence.

"They flashed down into a deadly vortex of fighting aircraft locked in mortal combat. Rolling, climbing, diving, spiralling all over the sky. You can imagine. Everyone's eyes glued to the gunsight, firing like crazy, all guns blazing as soon as they were in range. He told me it really was a pitched battle – kill or be killed!"

He paused, almost out of breath, reliving it.

"When his ammo had gone, my brother, called them all to return to base. Three of them landed safe, absolutely shagged but feeling bloody marvellous! Before debriefing they did a quick check. It looked like about five kills and they were still alive. Not bad, not bad at all. Of course it had to be confirmed. Charlie number two was not back yet, but he would show up somewhere sooner or later; the three of them certain about that.

But my brother's Number Two who'd made the warning call, saving them all, had disappeared. Somewhere, out in the channel, after his call, he'd gone down. Later in the day Group Headquarters confirmed that he was missing, presumed dead. My brother told me that he felt a piece of him had died too."

We all listened in silence, thinking that this was the end of the story, but there was more…

"Anyway, some time after that scrap over the channel when Charlie Number Two disappeared, my brother was scrambled to meet another raid building over the French coast. He said it was a real big one. But the weather was really bad. Huge cu-nimbs were building across the flight path of the raid, great masses of boiling cloud – weather to be avoided at all costs.

My brother had three enemy bombers lined up in his sights, range closing fast, their return fire all around him but no hits. He knew this was going to be a bonanza. Waiting, watching, closer and closer he got, but to his bitter disappointment his targets vanished into the sanctuary of the biggest black cu-nimb he'd ever seen, safe from his firepower. He broke hard to port, wrenching his plane around to avoid the turmoil he knew would be inside that whirling mass of cloud, but it was too late, its destructive force sucked him in. Soon the cloud had him in its grip, thrashing and tearing at his Hurricane, overwhelming and confusing his senses. He had no idea whether he was going up, diving down, moving sideways or any other orientation. He panicked. He could think of only one way to escape its merciless destruction. Struggling, he started to undo his seat harness with the intention of trying to bale out of his Hurricane.

'At that precise moment' he said, 'there was an eerie, calming spectre in the void around me, arresting my tumbling mind for a fraction of a second. Then I swear I heard a voice saying "Wait, Charlie, wait!"

For the smallest measure of time my whole being stopped. I couldn't think. Then as if by some miracle I broke from the bottom of the cloud mass with just enough clearance above the sea to pull back hard on the stick into straight and level flight and return to base. Of course there was no one else there, but, by all the gods, I swear my old friend Charlie had saved my life yet again'"

He finished his story and we sat silently for a moment or two, not sure whether to believe him or not. We were all too embarrassed to say our usual kind of response, along the lines of "what a load of rubbish!" Before anyone could venture anything at all he completely silenced us.

"My brother was killed about two months after he told me his two Charlies story."

I made my excuses and left, being on the first sortie out in the morning.

CHAPTER 4

Falling Down to Earth

The Ops signal directed us to carry out a strafing sweep along the railways from Edessa to Verria then to Llanovergi and Eleatherokhorion on the west coast of the Gulf of Salonika. The powers that be had allocated the sortie to two of us. It was going to be a testing day out there across the sea and Albania trying to find what we could find. I wondered what the day would hold for us.

As we headed up to our room – shared with all the members of the squadron on detachment – I thought of how it was when I first arrived in Brindisi, the excitement at being back in civilisation again, way out of proportion to the change, and an expectation of something I hadn't quite identified. Perhaps it was having service people outside the squadron around us; perhaps it was the women... Control Commission and Special Service girls with long wavy hair, cotton shirts that bulged in all the right places and skirts that moved seductively over hips that swayed when they walked; tantalising for all of us. Back at base we never even spoke of women, all thought of them suppressed in the cause of our lives dedicated to aeroplanes and war. It was less painful to accept that women had no part in our wartime world. I hadn't seen anything like these girls since I had said a sad farewell to my young wife of only a few weeks – in what now seemed a faded memory. Just looking at them surreptitiously had a stirring fascination; seeing them around was a kind of mental embarrassment. Thank goodness they could not read my unfaithful thoughts!

However, they were all too aware of their exaggerated scarcity value, which caused every one of them to be perceived as a great deal more glamorous than the eye beheld. They were in huge demand and they knew it. The place was alive with predatory males seeking their attention and their favours; they could pick and choose as they pleased. Unfortunately, the danger of our lives compared with the more comfortable existence of the local-based chaps, sitting in safety behind office desks, had no currency with the ladies. We looked and fantasised and envied, lacking the courage to have a go, too shy to even speak to them.

As soon as I opened the room door I sensed, more than heard, some kind of a conspiracy going on in the darkness. Several squadron pilots were bunched up around our big sash windows overlooking a courtyard between the two wings of our building. They were whispering in hushed tones and seemed transfixed by something happening in the building across the courtyard.

"Keep the light out!" they called, quietly, as I entered.

I joined them, wondering what it was all about.

"What's going on?"

"Have a look at THAT!" one of them invited.

Across the courtyard proved to be the women's quarters. Their identical widows faced ours on the same level. As we watched with fascinated eyes two girls came into the room, switched on the lights and slowly undressed, moving around as they did so, almost like a strip tease show, until one of then stood in full view, completely naked against the light, admiring the beauty of her body in a long mirror. As she examined her own natural charms at considerable length we watched breathlessly in highly excited admiration of all there was to be seen not more than 30 yards from us. Her back was to us with a full frontal reflection in the mirror. She was a wonderful sight in the extreme, the loveliest I had ever seen. She turned first this way, looking closely at her reflection, and then that way, without any apparent consciousness of the big open windows and the bright light shining on her as she stood there, a female revelation beyond description, a heart-throbbing sight, lovely breasts, high and firm, slightly bronzed nipples proud and prominent on delicate pink flesh, the kind of inviting youthful shape we could only dream about, curving down into her waist, delicately and smoothly rounding out again into the most inviting hips imaginable a triangle of soft black hair showed clearly between her long legs. It was a glorious sight for our sex-starved eyes. Hard to believe she was not conscious of our admiring presence so close across that open space between our rooms.

Suddenly the show was over and she disappeared into a bedroom. I felt a sense of Peeping Tom guilt.

"That's court martial stuff" I croaked, embarrassed at having to admit my guilt.

"Rubbish!" scoffed one of the chaps who had been there on detachment longer than any of us. "She does it regularly. I'm bloody sure she knows she's putting on a show; happens frequently. You've got to admit it. That's as close to heaven as you'll ever get!"

He went on to tell us that on a previous detachment they had all been glued to the window, sheltered by darkness, fascinated, watching the undressing scene as it unfolded before their very eyes, nearly crawling up the wall in their sex starved excitement. Suddenly some fool switched on the room lights. There was pandemonium. Everyone exposed at his nasty Peeping Tom worst, withdrawing from view with a speed to be envied by the Mustangs, not knowing if they'd been seen.

"And you're telling me that young lady doesn't know what's going on?"

One of them closed off the nights excitement saying, "Its a funny thing about women! When you see them like that you can see where you came from and why you spend the rest of your life trying to get back there!" We all laughed at him and hit the sack for the night. It may not have been a fully sexual rewarding experience, but I had to agree it was better than we knew at base camp – and far, far better than nothing! Tomorrow was not a long way off. After my blood pressure had reduced to near normal again and gorgeous women had been replaced in my thoughts by the reality to come, I mentally drifted, half asleep. No place for women out there. All we had to do was find some unlucky targets, blast them to pieces and get back across that long reach of hostile territory safe and in one piece. We had already lost quite a few chaps on sweeps out over the area;

tomorrow we'd have to take our chances, like everyone else who went that way. There was no way of predicting what was to come or how you would handle it when it did come. I closed my eyes and was asleep in no time at all.

The first thing I knew was a heavy shake on my shoulder.

"Time to get up, Mate. The pick-up will be here for us in about thirty minutes." He was to be my leader for the operation.

The truck had a feeling of cold hardness driving from the comforting warmth of our Mess to the flight line. We said nothing, each wrapped in silent thought quietly wondering what this day held. The briefing and the aircraft checks were quick and to the point. We strapped in, started up and taxied for take-off together. It went smoothly, we climbed to height and set course in battle formation, just the two of us in a lonely dawn sky. We headed out over a still-dark Adriatic Sea, crossing a lifeless Albanian terrain below. Small pockets of layered cloud still patched over the ground, here and there, resisting the rising sun that would melt them away later on. We reduced height down to operating level.

We flew on, following the route as briefed, searching, eagle-eyed through the mist shrouding the plain below for anything moving. Down to fifteen hundred feet, both of us sensitive to being at ideal light flak height, but higher up we might miss what we were hunting for in the semi-light of the gathering dawn.

I caught in the corner of my eye a line of deadly tracers weaving a pattern up to us from a railway siding. They knew we had arrived. The warning message would sweep ahead as we progressed. It was a close call. My pulse wound up. Miraculously everything seemed OK. The engine purred and all the instruments registered normal, but we'd been warned, they were not sleeping down there. I dropped back into trailing line astern allowing for a follow-up attack if my leader spotted something.

Suddenly his voice stormed into my earphones, with an excited message, words tumbling together in his urgency to get them out.

"Airfield – four o'clock – TWO AIRCRAFT ON IT. Going round to attack – follow me – keep low!"

I couldn't believe my ears. What was he saying? Aircraft? Down there for our taking. It was too good to be true. My pulse rate went up even higher. I pushed the engine wide open, made sure the gun trigger was switched to FIRE and swept around after him. Any fear of flak vanished in my complete concentration on what was coming. We sped on, staying as low as safety would allow, and I saw the airfield come into view as I made my wide ground-hugging arc, increasing my spacing line astern, getting the rising sun behind me. We were both eager for the kill; two kills. Ahead I saw his guns fire, stirring up a whole hornet's nest of flak. Yes, there it was coming from every corner of the ground below, black puffs, colour tracer, the bloody lot. We both knew that airfields were the highest risk target; the Germans would never expose their few remaining planes, always protecting them fiercely. Instinctively, I knew that this was going to be a real hairy one. Suppressing my almost overwhelming tension I called, "Flak – flak – flak!" (as if I needed to tell him) "stay down low on the run out!", my heart almost bursting with excitement and apprehension. I saw smoke and a mess of dust kick up ahead, the Leader's guns still going. We were almost too low for safety; the ground blurred past. I waited for the leader to clear my line of sight. I was too close. It was very tight for the flak gunners to get me in a steady alignment and I hoped they'd not have time to re-sight on me at this screaming speed, flat on the ground. In a blink of the eye, there they were, the light blue silhouettes of a pair of parked Folke Wolf 190s. Even in that split second the sleek outlines were pleasing to see. Two of them – PR jobs, I knew it, cockpit canopies sparkling in the early morning sunlight. I squeezed on the trigger grip exploding my point fives all over the place, slightly too flat for a perfect shot but knowing I'd score some hits.

The world around me flashed by in fractions of seconds; there was no measurement, no conscious registering of time and event, only instinct prevailed. I thought I saw the first 190 smouldering, the second taking the first bursts from my six, point five guns: tracer, armour piercing, all I had would be hammering at those two beautiful planes, jumping over engine cowling and cockpit, full force. The space between aiming, firing, and flashing over them came within only two or three breaths of pent-up tension.

A nightmare of ground armament erupted from every angle of vision below me, a brightly coloured chaos of light, each curving tracer trail marking a projectile seeking to find me, their menacing and patterns and colours almost mesmerising. Bigger black puffs, exploding separately, were the heavier bastards. How could they be missing me? There was no time for real thinking. I called again, not sure whether I had pressed the transmit button, wanting to release some of my pent-up stress.

"Keep low – KEEP LOW – flak everywhere!" I shouted, uselessly, against the roaring sound of my engine and the pounding heart beat in my ears, rocketing just clear of the trees, all ground detail an almost fluid stream of speed.

Thinking I must be clear of the airstrip and the two Fokker Wolf targets I hauled back on the stick, zooming for height away from the hornet's nest of flak. I'd never go back to something like that, however strong the temptation; so many of our chaps had been lost in second attacks, even when the targets appeared defenceless.

Scanning the sky for my leader I flew on, looking for more targets, shivering, trying to calm myself down a little, trying to think straight, concentrating on whatever was to come but feeling a glow of real success – I knew I was going to claim two FW190s 'severely damaged'. They had to be 'flamers' in order to claim them as 'destroyed', but I was not going back to confirm that, not for any price!

Our unexpected success showed me what being a fighter pilot was all about: chancing your arm on any opportunity that presented itself; risking all without thought; going beyond the limits of safety and feeling the exhilaration that comes from knowing you have achieved something at the margins of your ability, beyond that fringe of winged fear where the senses are electrified by the possibility of instant death.

Slowly I calmed down, throttling back, still scanning ahead for the leader. What a fantastic thing it had been... but I was still flying alone and above hostile territory; no time for thoughts of triumph. My sweeping eyes suddenly fixed on the port side of the engine cowling in shocked horror. A thin stream of white vapour was whipping back over the clear perspex of my cockpit canopy. I needed no second warning and felt a terrible surge of fear, not wanting to see it – a glycol leak – a slow wasting into the atmosphere of precious fluid vital to cooling my aircraft's engine. My radiator must have been damaged; punctured by flak. With all my might I willed that thin white ribbon to stop; eyes fixed on it. Gradually the tell-tale signs increased, spots of fluid coming with it, splashing onto the perspex surface. It was happening to me, now, my time had come. I sat for an instant bewildered, wondering what was to be done. Down there below I could see nothing but lifeless countryside, a long way from base and the familiar security I knew and wanted.

Now painfully aware of the inevitable outcome, I pushed the transmit button, trying to control the pitch of my voice to hide my anxiety.

"Blue One – I've been hit – climbing for altitude – can you see me? I'm setting course for the mountains."

It was a message I had always dreaded having to send. I felt a void of pain in my middle, a sinking feeling, but it was also a time of commitment; I had to act now – on my own. My message reached him, but there was nothing he could do to help me; it was all up to me now.

Until now it had just been a question of going out, flying the briefed operation, destroying the targets and returning to the safety of my base – forget about anything or anyone on the receiving end of my attacks – after all, I was only doing what I had been ordered to do. Now all the rules of the game had changed. I was suddenly vulnerable. Would there be any chance of making my way back to base from here? Determined to live, I nursed the stricken engine. Perhaps it could get me there after all.

The leader closed in to have a closer look at my damage. He moved around, trying to find a wound in the fuselage, a flaw in my great fighting bird. Anxiously, I waited on his word, desperate to hear his voice say, "nothing to worry about," confirming all was well; that we could make it together.

I was still clawing for height, reaching through ten and slowly up to fifteen thousand, thinking to get above any harm from down there below, aiming for the foothills, knowing my chances of survival would be better if I could find the partisans, hoping against hope that I would not have to bale out after all…

The sinister white plume thickened noticeably, spraying the precious liquid my plane needed to stay airborne. I levelled off, being careful not to overheat the engine, throttling back to cruising power and revolutions. How far could I get? Maybe all the way home, nursing my plane, listening for any changes in engine noise, examining every engine instrument three times more than necessary. 'PLEASE!' I thought, 'PLEASE GOD! Don't let it fall now!'

The Leader was still in close, circling round me, not finding enough to report, keeping me in suspense. I wanted to call him but didn't, not wanting to hear his reply unless it was to say something reassuring, but the instruments were registering the signs I knew to be terminal. The big Merlin engine up front, my lifeline to safety and to survival, coughed, and spluttered three or four times as if saying, 'This is my end'. All the coolant fluid was gone; it was overheating to death. The four powerful blades of my propeller wound slowly down and stopped in a terrible stillness as the engine seized up, completely dead. Suddenly it was menacingly quiet, with only the sound of the rushing airstream replacing the powerful throb of Merlin power. My sleek, silver Mustang III shuddered in its death throes at the point of stall as I unwisely tried holding height for a few more precious seconds. I knew it was now. The time was now. I must get out. Leave it – quickly, NOW.

I pushed the nose down to maintain flying speed above the stall. I made my last call, a lonesome and forlorn voice shouting against the roar of the increasing airstream.

"I've got to go out Blue One. I've got to bale out now!"

I was tugging frantically at the canopy release, smashing upwards with all my strength to make it go. It had been my protection, now it was a barrier to my survival. Now that it had no power, this beautiful aircraft with all its technical precision and aerodynamic efficiency had become a death-trap, a useless thing to be cast aside. I worked desperately to rid myself of it, to sever all connections with it. Bashing and thrashing wildly the canopy whipped away with a startling rush of sound. A bewildering maelstrom of blasting air swept everything sense aside, filling my cockpit, engulfing me. Its force disoriented my senses. I was no longer in control, my judgement gone. What was I to do to survive it?

"Its gone – GONE – going out now…" I shouted as loud as I could to overcome the forces around me, not knowing whether I had unplugged my R/T lead, concentrating with every fibre, everything flaying around me: helmet leads, oxygen tube – I had to focus, remember the drills! The slow, logical wisdom of training sessions in the safety of a warm classroom with an instructor intoning his disciplined knowledge flashed through my brain. In a kind of limbo between complete panic and the will to survive, I somehow did the things I was supposed to do. I thumped, releasing my seat harness and moved the stick violently across the pandemonium of my cockpit, rolling the dead Mustang onto its back. I let go and fell into the vast and terrifying emptiness of space…

It was a strange anticlimax. After the frantic struggle to escape from the cockpit and make decisions with the whole world whirling around me, I was suddenly as free as a bird. The soundless calm of a vacuum enfolded me: no restrictions, no encumbrances, no need to do anything, just be there, floating inertia-free in peace and quiet…

I snapped to my senses. All those drills proved their value again. My trained mind quickly dictated that I was in free fall and must judge when to pull the parachute D-ring. The terrain below looked as it always looked, completely devoid of life, a pattern of different coloured shapes, a winding pathway or two and beyond, patches of green, with trees in forest clusters. It all seemed small and far away as I fell towards it.

I fumbled for the D-ring of the ripcord to my chute, grasping and pulling with all my strength, not sure if I was the right way up, going sideways, or arse over tit. The D-ring came away surprisingly easily. For a fraction of a second I had a panic thought that nothing was going to happen. Then I heard a resounding WALLOP and felt a violent jerk as the harness between my legs and over my shoulders, snatched at my body, arresting my downward fall. The big canopy exploded into an umbrella shape above my head, ballooning out and swaying me from side to side. Grasping the shroud lines, I looked upwards into the great white mushroom, grateful for its protection against the first dangers of my descent into the unknown place below me.

I hung there, seemingly motionless in space, a tiny object in a big empty sky with time to look around and search for where I might land. It looked a harsh and unfriendly panorama, dry and hostile, drab and flat, spreading away endlessly in every direction as far as my eyes could see. All I could hear was the rushing of wind in the shroud lines and the occasional flap of the parachute panels, a strange and eerie quietness after the turmoil of baling out. I hung there, suspended, not unpleasantly, puzzled that there was no apparent closing with the ground, no positive sensation of falling through space at all. Yet falling I certainly was.

A flash across the sky, trailing a thin stream of white vapour, caught my eye. My big, silver, Mustang, was going down in a fatal, wide spiral, curving to its final destruction and death in the foothills down there. It had been delivered to the squadron only a few weeks previously, brand spanking new. Now it was moments away from ending as a mashed heap of metal in a big hole in the earth.

My descent seemed to go on and on without any indication that I was getting nearer to the ground. I wondered for a moment if I was actually falling – a stupid thought – I knew otherwise.

The sensation passed quickly. Foothills, down there, were taking on a shape. I could make out a pattern of cleavage between them and see shrubbery on the parched slopes. Suddenly it all started accelerating upwards towards me, the speed increasing with every blink. I grabbed at the shroud lines, trying to stop myself swinging, wanting to land going forward with the drift and uphill along one of the slopes. It was all happening too quickly for me to gain control.

I'd been lulled into a false sense of security as I fell. Now it was all panic again. I remembered to brace, with knees slightly bent, aiming to hit feet first, to roll sideways when I struck the surface, to break the initial force of an impact. I knew it was going to be a lot harder than the soft mat in the gymnasium in training. There was no time to think it all out. I had to do the proper things at the proper time – only one chance to get it right.

THUMP! The last few feet above the red earth vanished before I knew it, and I hit with the force and speed of a runaway train. My head whipped backwards, smacking into the ground almost severing it from my shoulders, a real black-out punch. I collapsed in a heap, dazed, giddy, feeling only half alive. The collapsing parachute followed, drifting past me, its lines tugging as it swelled in the wind, almost dragging me with its force. I knew enough not to release it too quickly and risk losing a valuable item of shelter I might well need later on. They'd said "Its bloody cold in the mountains, always hold on to your 'chute. You'll need it for more than one purpose." Labouring with every movement, feeling a searing pain across my head, I gathered in its billowing folds, heaping the silken tangle beside me. Hitting the quick release box I shed the harness. That was that! Groggy and vulnerable I sat on it. What to do now?

CHAPTER 5

Survival

A lifetime ago, way back at Advanced Flying Training School in Rhodesia, flushed with my own ability to fly and in the final stages of making the grade to be a pilot in the Royal Air Force, I'd spent an exciting weekend with kindly folk, on their vast cattle farm. Their daughter, a nubile lass of nineteen completely knocked me crazy; my first real love. She was more beautiful than anything I'd ever seen. I followed her around all weekend gaining confidence, getting bolder. I finally found enough courage to kiss her – a wondrous sensation. Still uncertain of her feelings towards me, my stay ended and we bid our fond farewells. She had said with an enticing chuckle, "Come and visit me in your aeroplane?"

I needed no further encouragement. Briefed for solo aerobatics in the following week, I made for the farm, showing her what a split-arsed fighter pilot I really was, breaking all the rules and regulations clearly laid down for U/T pilots. From below she stood on the front lawn, waving frantically at each pass I made overhead. The third and final one was my *piece de resistance* – low, almost touching the ground, I zoomed away and returned to base feeling a true knight of the air. On landing they found a large chunk of tree embedded in my port wing; they said it was 'major damage'. I was in deep disgrace, grounded and paraded before first, the OC Flying Wing, then in ascending order of judgement the Station Commander himself. It was to be the end of my flying career in the Royal Air Force, my treasured hopes of being a pilot dashed in one stupid act of flying disobedience. At both stages of the charge against Kings Regulations and all manner of illegal sins I invented and lied my way, refusing to admit to anything. Eventually the Station Commander, patience exhausted with trainee pilots trying to kill themselves, dismissed me, awarding a punishment less than my crime warranted, saying, "Alright young man, I know bloody well and so do you, you not only severely damaged one of our aircraft at risk to your own life but, you did it disobeying orders and beating up some girl friends place!"

I held my silence.

"Against my better Judgement I'm going to give you a second chance. Your flying reports are favourable. One day you might make a good fighter pilot. But above all remember this and remember it well – save your dashing spirits, your initiative, until you know what in hell you are doing!" I marched from his office wondering how I'd escaped decapitation.

Where oh where was my dash and initiative now? What was I going to do to get out of this one? My reasoning wandered around. I sat, full of indecision. Something had to be done, pain or no pain I had to move! But which way? Not downwards, the Germans must have seen me. Higher into the mountains above me? What was there? In shock, I remembered I hadn't eaten anything or had a drink since last night. I had to do something to stay alive. I stood up, my feet on the firmness of earth that sloped away in every direction, covered in sparse shrub surrounded by an uneasy vast stillness. Listening, I could almost hear the silence; no familiar sound came to me. The soft swishing of wind through the growth of trees was the only sound, there was nothing human, nothing I could relate to.

Trying to think, I pulled out the .38 revolver at my hip – all intact, fully loaded, pushing it back into the holster, buttoning down the flap. The small .22 automatic inside my flying boot was also still there. I knew I must be careful. If I met anyone with a gun in my hand it could spark a hostile response. Settle down, settle down! My mind swung from an urge to activity one moment to an overwhelming fatigue the next. Don't panic. Think it out. What had they told me about finding the partisans?

All measurement of time had been eclipsed – the events of earlier in the day seemed a long way off: our departure from base, setting course, searching for targets, sighting of the Focke Wolf 190s, the exciting attack in my Mustang, that traumatic escape into space, the heavy landing in this wilderness of nothing, the shock of it all. Now I was here and alone.

Gathering the folds of soft silk into a manageable bundle I hefted the parachute harness, my dinghy and survival pack onto my shoulder. The heave hurt like hell. Slowly I moved off the slope, treading warily across the treacherous surface, moving to my left, aiming for a less exposed clump of pines. Blowing like a horse with effort and some pain, I thought it out again. Yes, leave the revolver in the holster, they'd said that. "Don't meet friend or foe with a fist full of gun unless you decide to kill someone. It could develop a situation you don't want."

Climbing up the other side of the incline, towards the trees was heavy going. It would be easier to get rid of my chute, harness and dinghy pack, but they were valuable, I didn't want to do that. It was only some hundred yards upwards. I collapsed at the fringe thankful to have better shelter, relieved to put down the weight I was carrying. It was getting hot. I felt an uncomfortable dryness in my throat.

I stopped breathing. Concentrating, I thought I could hear voices in the clear air, distant but recognisable against the stillness around me. Nothing there… imagination? Then again the sound came with the wind. It changed everything. I came alive, standing to look, searching all around, trying to locate whatever it was. Uncertain of how I should react if anyone came into sight. Should I shout and draw attention, hope for the best? Should I wait quietly and see what came to me?

Then a movement on the skyline above the ravine and further up caught my eye. Emerging from a patch of shrubs was a dark skinned boy. He was looking for me. A young girl followed, her long dark hair swirling. Their keen young eyes quickly found and fixed on me. They both stood together, very still, childlike, staring at this stranger in their place. The one they'd been looking for. Obviously they had seen my parachute descent.

I looked at them; they looked at me, all of us uncertain about the next move. The sight of two children together was reassuring. They appeared harmless, making no move to show how they judged me. Together they came forward off the ridge as if to get a better view. They were dressed in raggedy clothes, bare footed, with olive skin complexions. Both smiled at me, big friendly grins. It was impossible not to smile back. Yet I was still doubtful. Could they be a kind of decoy for what was to come? The boy raised his arm, seeming to wave, testing the situation. Then he shouted, "Ingleese! Ingleese!" a shrill, friendly little voice. I couldn't be sure if it was a question or a statement being made to someone else out of sight. These children would not be alone.

"Yes, yes! Ya-ya! Ingleese!" I called back, not able to contain myself, feeling a surge of relief, thinking I had been found by someone who'd lead me to safety – out of this place of desolation. The vital help I wanted must be near at hand somewhere beyond those two kids. They made no move to come closer. A shadow of doubt crossed my mind. Was it really going to be OK? The boy went back to the top of the ridge, calling in a language I had never heard. I waited. A group of burly-looking chaps, five of them, came into view behind the lad. Two of them carried weapons, heavy looking shotguns. They slithered down the slope until opposite me, spilling loose rock and red dust as they came, talking aloud, showing excitement at seeing me but not coming closer.

A big chap in the group, his gun held at the ready, stood above them. Friendly they may be, but he looked to be taking no chances. Suddenly he called, silencing the others.

"Ya Ingleese?" followed by a stream of unintelligible words I would loved to have understood.

"Yes, yes, me Ingleese pilot – my plane shot down," I stammered, eager to tell them what they most certainly knew already. I left it at that. The next move must be theirs. Nothing came for a minute. They gabbled again seeming to decide who would do what. They gestured for me to stay were I was.

Two of them detached from the others coming to me in the trees. They moved quickly, rough looking characters dressed in a motley selection of clothes, rushing the last few yards, nearly overwhelming me. The first one grabbed my arms, encircling me in a powerful bear hug, his greeting spontaneous and warm. I could have been his long lost brother. As they each wrapped big muscular arms around my body their smell was as strong as I'd ever known. The others followed at a slower pace and coming down in turn each grasping my hand in two of theirs. They all had to do it, saying things I could not understand. Even the two kids. It was one of the greatest welcomes I had ever known! Minutes ago I had sat dejected wondering what was in store, hoping for a kind of miracle rescue. Now I knew these mountain men were my way to safety and to freedom again. I had found the guerrillas, the partisans. They were my friends. My heart felt fit to burst with relief. The good Lord had seen fit to save me.

The big chap pointed at my revolver showing he wanted me to take it off and hand it over. I shook my head and he appeared to accept the decision. The others gathered up my 'chute, the survival pack and the dinghy. Showing where we should go, pointing down the foothills, making signs that the Germans were coming. Slowly, walking at my laboured pace, we climbed upwards, going in the direction they had come from.

I climbed on in the middle of them feeling the steepness of the ascent. Slipping at almost every step. Two or three paces forward, two or three feet backwards, grasping whatever came to hand, the spindly shrubs or a helping hand. I was worrying how long I could keep going. Pilots were for flying aeroplanes not for cross-country obstacle journeys over impossible mountain slopes!

We went on for a short spell that felt to me like half the day had passed until I indicated to them that I wanted to stop and rest before my tired legs gave out, to catch my breath. I mimed that my head still ached from the parachute fall. The pain had almost disappeared in the excitement of being found, greeting them and feeling secure but now it was there again, a dull throb, perhaps concussion. My right leg was also giving me gip. I must have hit the ground on that side. They showed understanding, grouping around me, swapping information I could not understand. It sounded like sympathy. I tried sign language but nothing came of it. Just smiles and a shake of the head. The head man indicated I should sit with my back to a tree. He took my hand, lowering me to a sitting position. He had an iron grip but a beaming face went with it. The blueness of his eyes surprised me, they were piercing, crystal clear, full of camaraderie, impressive, powerful, his face tanned black by the sun. An enormous moustache completely hid his upper lip and his great head of tangled hair was held in place by a knitted, military-looking cap. They gave me a few brief minutes, exchanged words and in sign language indicated that there was no more time to lose, the Germans would be coming up from the plain to search me out. He drew a weathered black hand horizontally across his neck from ear to ear, exposed two rows of stained yellow teeth and threw up his two enormous palms, emphasising the kind of threat we might expect if we didn't move quickly on. He indicated that a German patrol had searched the village once before. They had travelled up the mountain trail in trucks, or something guided by a steering wheel, grabbed four villagers and taken them away. He swept two hands across his face, open palms outwards. They had disappeared. I wanted to prolong my rest but he shook his head. We must go on, up the steep gradient.

After a short distance we climbed out onto a rough mountain road hacked into the hillside, eroded away, scattered with outcrops of sharp stones and heavily rutted. The more I trod to avoid the sharp stones the more I felt them through the flimsy soles of my flying boots, which were not made for mountaineering. I laboured on, breathing hard and feeling less excited about being rescued and more anxious about my exhaustion. I knew I must be suffering from shock and I was tired, thirsty and hungry. But I had to keep going; they expected it of me. I was the hero of the day and they were helping me – but what was an everyday trudge for their mountain-toughened bodies was an endurance test for me. We climbed on for an hour or two, winding around corners, seemingly never getting any closer to our destination. Then, suddenly, surprising me, others appeared out in front of us. They must be other villagers coming down to see who I was. They stood, looking expectant, smiling in cautious greeting, saying words I couldn't understand but clearly directed at me. A few came closer to have a look, others standing further off but staring with interest at the novelty suddenly in their midst. Who was this intruder who'd burst into their world unheralded. I smiled back, waved a hand in greeting, gritted my teeth and kept going. It was not easy.

I had two problems now, an aching head and a painful right knee. I must keep going for as long as it took to ensure my survival and I had no idea how I was going to communicate with these people. I concentrated on keeping up with to their leader; I was puffing like a horse, lungs gasping for more oxygen as we continued. The air around us had a crisp and clear feel to it.

I marched on, placing one heavy foot after the other, slogging at it. I felt the wetness of cold sweat running down my back and beads of perspiration trickling from my aching head. I knew I must give in and demand another breather, sit down and refuse to budge until I'd caught my breath again, but his mimed warning about the Germans came to mind and I knew he hadn't been fooling.

Finally I reached the end of my tether. I just couldn't go on, knowing I was ready to drop because there was nothing left in my body. The chap leading us stopped and catching my eye indicated that the way ahead was flat, cut deeper into the slope, downhill even. He was pointing out to the left and saying something of importance. Following the direction of his arm I saw, to my great relief, through the pine trees ahead were the first scattered buildings of the village. 'Thank God for that!' I thought. It was almost as if I had been tested to my limits and given succour at the very last moment of my endurance. It was a sight for sore eyes and no mistake. I gave a huge sigh of relief and smiled at them. It was a happy scene again. They knew that I had almost 'had it'.

The village was only a rough, peasant-looking place, but it was a haven of rest for my exhausted spirits. I summoned enough energy to lift my shoulders and go on with a measured stride. The going down hill made things a lot easier. We rounded a corner and there before me was a place I'd never expected to see when I had taken off from Brindisi that morning, or at any other time of my life. It was all stones. The few buildings were spaced out haphazardly on either side of the narrow throughway, not really a road but made of smooth, round rocks with spaces between them for drainage, yellow and worn by countless generations of feet across the centuries. Animals were tethered here and there. The whole picture was of poverty but for me it also meant security... for the moment anyway.

CHAPTER 6

Salvation

Apart from the twenty or so people around me, the men who'd rescued me and the other curiosity seekers, the village looked deserted. I saw a couple of women carrying baskets; otherwise little or nothing. Smoke curled up from several houses, hanging in the still mountain air, an unspoken message that there was normal life going on out of sight. I stopped, pausing to look this strange place over, wondering about it, feeling extremely tired, hoping they'd take me somewhere I could lie down and rest. A handful of young children emerged, mongrel looking dogs jumping and yapping about them. They had got the message and wanted to see me for themselves. Shyly, they stood off gazing at me with unblinking eyes. They were poor and ragged looking, but they had a tangibly friendly quality I could relate to.

How was I to tell these people what I wanted? I was too tired to work it out and walked on. Taking their initiative from me they all started moving again. Uncertain about what to do next, I stopped at a place in the middle of the buildings that was probably the village square. I turned to the group immediately around me, held my hands in a questioning gesture and shrugged my shoulders as if to say, "What now?"

I need not have bothered. The big chap was already pointing to a large building close by. Though poor in structure, like the others, it boasted two floors and a flight of stairs leading up, and was in a commanding position fronting an open space. Going up those wooden steps was a real effort, my legs were heavy and pain was coming from my right knee. It was bare inside, just a rough-hewn table and a few chairs positioned centrally in the room. The big chap smiled and gesturing indicated I should take one. It was not difficult to oblige him and I flopped down into it. How bloody marvellous it was to take the load of my legs and weary feet.

Two of them brought my gear up and, thinking to assert my authority, I pointed, showing them to place it all in the corner. That stuff: the 'chute material and harness, my dinghy pack and the survival kit were valuables in this locale but nothing had been touched, it was all there, intact. I sat down again, embarrassed at being the prize exhibit for all to see and stare at, not able to say anything.

They were interested in my welfare and my comfort – they had already shown that – but they were restrained, unable to question me or tell me anything. A hell of a lot of friendly miming and gestures were going on but it was incomprehensible to me. I was no help: dazed, still suffering from shock, tired and hungry, I was struggling to adjust to all that had happened over the last dozen or so hours that had taken me from squadron life in Brindisi to this distant and rugged place. I could do little more than look blankly at them and feel empty and frustrated in my exhaustion and pain. Most of all I wanted them to leave me alone but I knew that was impossible. Perhaps half an hour passed while we sat there going through our animated pantomime. I managed to relive, for them, how I had shot up German planes, been hit by flak and baled out of my plane to land where they'd found me. At least, that's what I thought they understood from the sympathetic nodding of heads. It was some small reward for my efforts.

I was distracted by something of a commotion outside. Someone was climbing the steps. A short, overweight, man entered the room, showing some deference to the big chap sitting within our circle of chairs. He was a real swarthy-looking type with sparkling eyes and an air about him that said this was his moment. He looked at me, thumbs stuck into the waistband that girded a very ample belly, waved a hand forward and through a mouthful of stained teeth said, "Hello friend!"

Blessed be my luck, he was an English speaker! It was a very happy sound to my ears.

I rose to meet him, but my right leg gave way under me. He grabbed me and lowered my body into the chair. "Good, good, you sit there. You rest. I talk to you. You tell me." He shook my hand in a warm expression of his goodwill. The big guy said something and all was halted, without question.

"This the head man," said my English speaker. "He say we move all these peoples out and we talk here now."

They cleared the room of everybody but my interpreter, the headman and three others. It was obvious the headman was going to control things from now on. First of all, they wanted my full story. Where I was from? How had I got there? What was I doing? Did I know anything about the Germans down on the plain? What was happening in the war? A full session of questions and answers was laboriously translated. Apart from the main queries they never interrupted, accepting what I said, or at least that was how it appeared to me. Each time he translated they listened intently, watching my face as I spelled it out in the simplest possible terms. I thought I had said it all. The nods of heads showed it was well received. But they started asking more questions and it seemed to go on and on. So much to cover: the war, the British, the Americans, the Germans. Where were the armies? What where they doing? What was happening to Greece? What was going to happen? When would it happen? If I hadn't made most of it up as we progressed I would have been a disappointment to them. I answered everything they raised with the best level of informed ignorance at my command. Eventually I said "This is good, I am pleased to tell you anything but I am very tired. I have not had anything to eat or drink today. I am exhausted. It is a big thing to fly my aeroplane and be shot down. I am very tired." I did not add that I wanted to lie down and sleep and sleep and sleep…

The interpreter gave them the message. They nodded understandingly. Then the headman spoke.

"He says the Germans make searches up here, in this place and all the way along the villages here." He swept an arm out to indicate the world outside. "He says, you safe for now. His men watching for anyone coming. They see Germans they come tell him. They know you jump out of plane. Maybe they want find you. He not think they come today." His expression, his respectful gestures indicating where these words came from, seemed to add up to "here this head man's word is law." He went on, "They know your airplane where it crash. It two kilometres other side of hill. It a small walk. They says they take you see it. They wants we go and see. They wants we go and see now." Repeating, "It small walk. We back before dark tonight." He was at his persuasive best. The headman watching for signs to see what I might say.

I looked at him and shook my head in clear indication that I couldn't do it. It was impossible. "My head" and I tapped it for emphasis "is too sore" and reaching down I rubbed my open palms along my tired thighs, "my legs too much pain," shaking my head again. "Tomorrow, we can go and look in the morning. In the afternoon we go to the British Mission." Cleverer than I thought, I had a trade off. I'd meet their wish, take them to the crashed wreck of my plane, agree they could have it for scrap, if they'd take me to the British Mission. But did they know where the British Mission was? I had to get there so I could go back to my squadron in Italy and fight in the war again. He relayed it to them and an exchange continued for some little time.

But they were not to be side-tracked from their single-minded purpose of going to see that aeroplane crash site.

"They can have the aeroplane," I said palms open giving it away. But that was not the way of things. They were insistent. I must inspect the wreckage and approve its release to the headman, on the spot. Why they insisted on this type of sanction escaped me. Maybe they had some sort of partisan code, a chain of authority for doing things like this. The primitive setting of the village, the obvious poverty of the place in general could be misleading. The head man smiled ingratiatingly, speaking again through the interpreter,

"Yes, he says Mission long walk, maybe more than one day. They take you over the mountain to that place. First, now we eat, after we go see airplane, after then man take you to Mission. Maybe tomorrow."

He was going to win anyway. I nodded my head accepting the inevitable. A general murmur followed. Everything in ordered sequence, just what they wanted.

Andreas, as he was called, spoke an aside to me, possibly risking censure. It was clear he did not rate very highly in this gathering but his presence and his knowledge of English were vital. He said they would never let me move from the village until the word came from higher up the partisan chain of command. He couldn't tell me how or when this might happen but it was how things worked around here.

"They is the big shot. They do whichever they like. We not do it this place before they say so. When OK come – OK."

That was that and I could not take it further. The four others showed they did not think much of our aside conversation that excluded them. Asking him what I was saying. He looked to be brushing it aside as nothing much.

A bottle appeared with six little glasses on a wooden tray. They invited my attention showing it was for my approval, indicating hospitality time had arrived. The headman spoke and each small glass was filled to capacity. The tray went around, first to me, as though this was some kind of special treat, nectar from the mountains of the gods. I took one as expected and sniffed it. The strong aroma from the liquid almost singed my nostrils, stinging my eyes. They watched my every move. I tested the smell again with more caution, smiling an un-tasted approval. This was surely meant to be a gesture of hospitality to cement the bonds of brotherhood between us. They motioned, indicating the correct procedure. Up-end the lot, one swift gulp down. It would be good. Smiles all over their faces.

"You drink – Sir. *Very* good," heavily emphasising the *very* part of it. "Make from best grape. You drink down – one quick time – that best way."

I smiled my doubts. They all grunted, nodding heads, reinforcing what he said without knowing the meaning of it. There was no way out of this one. I knew well what was to be done and I knew well I did not want to do it.

Taking a deep breath, bracing my long since empty stomach, not wanting to offend, I put the little innocent glass to my lips, tossed back my head and swallowed. Instantly I knew it was the biggest mistake of my short life. My nervous system seized in revulsion, stomach contracting against the burning fire. The liquid was sheer dynamite. Catching my breath, feeling its almost instant effect, I coughed and spluttered, much to their delight. I sat paralysed with the burning sensation in my throat and gullet waiting for the spasm to pass, to regain control. A miraculous warmth slowly suffused through my body. The dull pain in my head vanished, I forgot about my knee. I was a being brought back to life again. Lovely! The exhaustion gone I sensed a kind of rejuvenation.

They looked expectant, weather worn faces wrinkling in curiosity as if asking "Now, how did you find that, my friend?"

I found it most welcome and I showed them, saying, "That's very good stuff, very strong. I like it." They laughed their approval, exchanging glances as if to say 'he's human, like us!' The taste was awful but the effect was electrifying. They indicated that I must have a follow up, one more small glass, good for me after my day's ordeal, waving aside my weak protest, dismissing my indication that it made me feel dizzy in the head. Of course, it was supposed to have that effect on me. Slowly I sipped at the glass with experienced caution. Perhaps not the traditional way to drank it but definitely the best for my vulnerable constitution. There were no objections. They accepted me as different anyway.

When they judged I had been suitably softened, alcoholically mellowed, they started asking questions about my safety equipment. Bringing each item into the centre of the room, placing everything in a valuable pile on the bare boards in front of me. This was meant to suggest it was mine but they would like to know about it.

Andreas had been well briefed for his part to play. Soft smiles, a kind of beguiling friendliness, he started lifting up my survival pack, "You safe now, Sir. Soon you go over mountain to British Mission. If you kindness you give these peoples these things?" Throwing an all embracing band to indicate the whole lot, dropping the survival pack, going to each item in turn, showing he was talking about all of them, not just any one thing.

Then pointing at my. 38 in its canvas green holster. "They need the guns for fighting when after you gone." He even remembered to include the .22 automatic I had shown them in my flying boot. "This one very good, they like special much." His words lacked the sound of a question. More, they were telling me through him what was required of me and what I had brought into their miserable midst.

I remained silent, a non-committal shrug of the shoulders, an expression on my face that said, 'no'. At the same time, alcohol or not, I felt vulnerable in their hands, my life under their control. Would I ever be missed? Would I ever be traceable if I disappeared? It had happened and I knew it. He changed his tactics slightly explaining that the parachute, the dinghy and survival packs had done their turn. I would not need them again, now I was safe. His idea about being safe caught my attention. If they were saying things like that, surely I was a lot safer than I thought; little to worry about.

For the guns he spoke in pleading voice, squeezing hands together almost in supplication. No doubt these were the true objects of desire by the headman. He might have said 'get those for me and you will be rewarded'. Not receiving the response he'd hoped for he suddenly changed his request.

"You not want TWO guns. You have small gun. These peoples nice to you, you give other gun?"

I compressed my lips and shook my head firmly showing they could not have my guns. Then as a gesture I conceded, "Yes, I do not need the parachute or harness and they can have my dinghy and my survival pack," pushing at each item with my flying boot toe. "I keep them until I leave for the British Mission. The dinghy I will blow up and use to sleep on, the parachute will keep me warm and I want some of the things inside this one" I indicated the survival pack, "for my journey to the British Mission." I couldn't have carried any of it anyway. Not across the mountains. I wasn't sure I had much choice and after all, these guys had saved my life.

There was general all round approval once my words were translated, gleams of satisfaction behind their black bushy moustaches. Food began to appear. They said it was special for me. I should eat.

Eat! I thought. I had not done that for far too long ago. Still in mellow mood from the powerful liquid in those small glasses, I looked at the large communal dish in the centre of the table. They gave me a plate and a spoon, inviting me to attack it. Hunger or not, first impressions were not good; nothing familiar in any of it, nothing at all, just a pile of dull-brown mash. Goat, grain and herbs they said. A treat for me to enjoy? But eat it I must and like it, that I knew. They waited for me to transfer what I wanted from the main plate and piled in themselves until it had all disappeared.

I started tentatively, showing pleasure. A great feast? The smell of it wrinkled my nose, the taste flat and slightly bitter – but it was food. Eating would help me feel better.

That same morning, over all those compressed hours ago, I had left the Mess in Brindisi where the usual fatty early morning breakfast food was available, served on a plate at a table with a white cloth, serviettes, knives and forks, a cup of tea in a civilised dining room. Now it was this slightly repulsive mess or nothing – the choice needed no hesitation. Whether I liked the taste or the smell of it my empty stomach received it gratefully and I felt better.

They wasted no time on preliminaries, "We go see airplane now. Little walk – we be there."

I had no way to resist; I had been offered the best they had now they wanted only this in return. We walked beyond the village and down through a ravine, scrambling up the side of a steep slope, showering pine and flint shale as we progressed. Our route followed a worn trail and the going was easier than I had expected, but the last mile or so tested the remnants of my endurance again. They kept me at it, shouting encouragement, offering a helping hand when needed. For them it was some kind of pleasure outing; for me it was extremely demanding on legs and lungs. Every pause or hesitation had them pushing or shouting me on.

Finally, after clambering up a very steep gradient that took all I had left, we emerged onto a wide and flat plateau. Pointing, they indicated that this was where my Mustang had fallen. It was needless indication. An open area had been blasted and torn apart with the terrible violence of the plane's impact. Dirt and stones had been flung wide and the shrub growth ripped by the explosion. Right in the centre of the plateau, as though deliberately aimed, was a big hole and what remained of my Mustang III. The sight of it was spectacular enough to shock me; a terrible, twisted and tangled mess of shredded silver metal, coloured wires, glass, perspex, wheels, tyres, engine parts, everything. Beyond recognition as the sleek fighter plane I had flown that morning.

Looking down at the warped and jumbled chaos had me shaking my head in disbelief. Surely this was not the fighter plane I had sat in, thrilling to the destruction of those two Luftwaffe Focke Wolf 190s, just a few hours ago? The time lapse was short to absorb. It was a saddening sight, the compacted fuselage, just recognisable lay buried five feet down. They told me they had heard the explosion when it hit, over two miles away in the village. A lump came to my throat. Bits and pieces of it were everywhere across the damaged and destroyed area of the plateau. Armour piercing, tracer and high explosive point five ammunition had projected upwards and outwards. Some of it still in linkaged belts, mostly single bullets, yellow brass shining bright in the evening sunlight. It was clean looking, alive, still dangerous and probably sensitive.

For a moment I fought back the tears, surprised at my own feelings. It was an impersonal thing after all, just a machine, yet that plane had been a wondrous thing, created with great precision, at a high cost, cleverly fitted together, a complex design of metal, wires, tubes, hydraulics, electrics, guns and explosives with a powerful engine and four-bladed prop that raced it through the air; a gleaming silver marvel! And it had been *mine,* with my own emblem painted on the side of the cockpit, a kind of extension of me. Alas, it was no more now.

More times than I could remember I'd flown this plane out over the Adriatic Sea the land masses around it, dived my two five-hundred pound bombs into a target with showers of deadly bullets following. How my spirits had soared whenever I'd slipped into that cockpit, started up the engine, checked the instruments and taken off with the others, always the promise of excitement to come, tinged with that sensation of fear I knew before each operational mission. With the sheltering carapace of the clear cockpit canopy around me I would enjoy unrestricted vision, stretching away to every point of the compass. Strapped in and secure I would sit, absorbing the information from the orderly spread of neat-looking dials and gauges, coloured and marked to alert if anything was wrong, gripping the American-style control column, reassuring and neat, the trigger for the guns under my thumb. I remembered the feeling of those six guns recoiling through the airframe as I fired on those FW190s that very morning, an unbelievable lifetime away. That beautiful thing was now a heap of useless, expensive scrap. I walked away from it, knowing that they would not understand my thoughts. To them it was a treasure house of valuable material to be salvaged, turned to good purpose, used in any way their innovative powers could invent; a gift from the gods.

I could feel them watching me, waiting for my reaction.

"Take it, take the whole bloody thing!" I said, sweeping my arm to indicate the entire area of scattered debris. The time would come when they'd forage and salvage whatever could be taken. Only God knew whether in doing so the ammunition spread far and wide, would explode and take off someone's arm or leg, but that was their worry...

Fatigue returned. I felt heavy. The light was fading into evening. The leaden feeling of exhaustion returned like a weight upon me. I indicated that I wanted to return to the village, knowing I could do nothing more in my dejected state of mind. What the hell! At least I was safe in their hands. Going back the way we'd come was easier, most of it downhill. An old villager passed me on his way up to the crash site – maybe he was going to guard it. By chance I glanced at his feet and was astonished to see that his sandals were made from Mustang tyre material. Amazing! How quickly they could take advantage of an unexpected opportunity like that.

The headman, walking behind me, shouted at him, stopping us all in our tracks. There was an exchange of heated words. It appeared to be about the newly acquired footwear. They were at it for longer than I needed. I left them, continuing on with two of the others. Later, Andreas told me the old chap in sandals was in big trouble.

"They shoot him, maybe? He steal it. That bad thing."

I was so surprised and I cried "No-no!" shaking my head to make him understand it would be wrong, "That plane, all the things up there. They can have that. Don't let anybody get shot for that!" Then I let it go. What they did under their own village or partisan codes was nothing to do with me. I couldn't imagine it happening anyway.

"We hide you in special place now. You sleep safe tonight."

They led me to a cellar hidden below the village house. It was black, and slightly damp with a single candle. I made sure all my survival gear went with me. Inflating the dinghy with a billowing whoosh I showed them I had a bed with the 'chute for covering, a bit short on length but good cushioned comfort against the bare stone floor. After they left I remembered that I'd failed to ask why I was being hidden away. Surely the Germans would not come at night – if indeed they came at all. I only hoped the village men would find me when the time came in the morning!

Too tired to worry about anything now I lay in the corner of the cellar, wrapped the soft silken folds around me and quickly dropped into the depths of blissful oblivion.

Coming to in the black dankness I wondered, momentarily, where I was. Reality quickly replaced my passing uncertainty. I felt and fumbled my way to the door, forcing it open. The first light of a new day met me with blinding shafts of brightness. I blinked it away, hoping this would be the day when I would be off to the British Mission. I felt rested, and breathing in that special kind of clean fresh air one only gets in the mountains it seemed that this was a day full of promise. My head still had a soft floating feel to it, sensitive, not quite right, possibly concussion? My right knee felt sound. Thank God my legs were OK and ready for the journey to come. They'd take care of me, I felt sure about that. The tales about rival Greek factions crossed my mind. There were stories about manoeuvring for supremacy when the Germans pulled out. What had Spy troubled to brief us about? There was a pro-German faction and one allied to the British through Missions behind German lines. If the wrong lot got you they would hand you over to their women for special attention "They'll cut off your balls and sew them into your mouth!" he had said. I had to chuckle, stuff and bloody nonsense! Anyway, I was sure that had been about Tito's lot and the Chetniks in Yugoslavia. These were the Greeks and friendly.

I strolled around the village, stretching my legs, nodding to the occasional encounter and climbed the steps to their centre house. They gave me black bread of unknown origin and hot water for my survival tablets. It was a good breakfast. Thinking it out, chewing at the tough stuff in my mouth, I knew I had to keep their main interest focussed on me, to sustain my hopes of leaving this harsh mountain environment as soon as I could. Certainly, I was safe and pretty healthy, but I was blind about what was to come. Yesterday they'd said the Germans were still in the Salonika area and south east on the plains beyond the foothills from the village, a long haul for any motorised unit, and the prize of my capture too small for them to bother with.

Andreas was nowhere to be seen. When I asked for him, the head man shook his head, shrugged his shoulders, motioning me to sit and relax and do what I found most difficult – nothing at all! They knew more than I did but there was no way of finding out. It was frustrating not to be able to talk. How was I going to persuade these chaps I should be taking off now? It was a long day. They were quite happy for me to stroll around the confines of the village, but always within sight.

In a single embarrassing mime I showed them I needed to shit. Ah yes! They knew what I was after, leading me to a square hole in the ground hidden behind two walls abutting the centre house. It required a careful aim and one of my flight maps to satisfy the call of nature.

The evening meal, much the same as my first unpalatable experience, was quickly followed by another night's sleep in the cold comfort of my dungeon, but sleep I did and very well! Thinking out how I night insist on a departure the following day, I woke and walked up to the centre for another go at the black bread and survival tablets, indicating as best I could what I had to do. They nodded away, talked among themselves, working it out, telling me in unknown words what they had to say. Although we seemed to make little progress, I was getting the message that this day would bring something forth. It did.

About half way through the morning, a big, rugged-looking character, more of a soldier type in bearing and dressed better than the villagers came to me. He carried a rifle, a sure sign of authority around here. He said we would go to the British Mission. The message was music to my ears. I asked him when and he indicated 'right now'. All my anxieties vanished at a stroke. Here was the man who would get me back to civilisation and my Squadron. I told him to wait and went looking for the headman, but he already knew about my guide before I got to him. It was going to be difficult without Andreas to help. The guide spoke to the headman when I indicated, 'You tell him.' It all seemed to go OK, although I had no way of knowing what actually passed between them.

These people in their isolated village had rescued me at a time when I was at my lowest ebb. They had fed me and secured my safety. The crashed Mustang was not much repayment. Nodding his head the headman acknowledged the gift of my parachute and harness, my inflated dinghy, with its paddles and canopy and what was left from my survival kit after I had plundered it for my own immediate needs. My heart went out to them. They had so little, yet in their poverty they had been wonderful to me. I shook his hand and without thought unbuckled my .38 revolver, holster and ammunition pouch attached, handing it to him. He took it, an unexpected look of gratitude and surprise spreading across his rugged face. He clasped me in a breathless bear hug. That was it. I motioned to the guide and off we walked without goodbyes or ceremony.

Reaching the top of the steep slope, I turned, looking back and feeling I'd left something important behind. Their lives and mine had been entangled for a brief two days, thrown together by the fortunes of war, and now we parted, our paths in life never to cross again.

"Goodbye, Kegala Livadia," I muttered. A few of them who were still standing watching our departure waved a farewell. I returned it in thanks for their having saved my hide, and drew the curtain on act two in my survival drama.

Village scene, Kegala Livadia, Greece, 1944.

CHAPTER 7

Coming Down the Mountain

I ran to catch up with my guide, impatient to reach our destination. Over the first few miles, through hours of steady walking, head down, concentrating on the going, the path was even, almost level. I kept his pace without a problem, occasionally looking to admire the wonder of the autumn canopy of trees around us. There was colour and a silence such as I had never heard. It was completely quiet, a mountainous emptiness indifferent to our passing intrusion, not even so much as the flutter of a bird disturbed by our progress. The day went on, one foot in front of the other, never stopping. It was getting tougher with each passing hour. Eventually I shouted at him to stop for a rest. Reluctantly he nodded in agreement, indicating that we still had a long way to go, the distance important to my escaping the Germans, who could be behind us and following. It was not a convincing argument, not here in this enveloping peace with its umbrella of trees, but he had the advantage over me, knowing where we were going, how long it would take and when we would get there. I asked him how long? He shook his head, waved a hand forwards, indicating our journey should continue towards our unknown destination, so on we went again. It was the longest walk I'd ever known or wanted to know. Suddenly, as we were crossing a small stream he motioned me to stop and sit, offering a small bunch of sweet black grapes, and a broken-off handful of coarse black bread. Putting my face in the running clearness of the stream, I relished the ice cold sting of the mountain water, the taste sweet and freezing in my mouth and down my throat; it was refreshing nectar.

We got up again after ten minutes and walked on. He did not seem to know that RAF fighter pilots were not trained like mountain goats and built for marathon endurance! He kept me at it, walking slightly ahead, not slacking speed whatever the gradient of the path. Our rests grew shorter and the distances between them longer. He switched to walking behind me as if to prod my weary limbs along, intimidating, ensuring the pace did not slacken. No stopping, no making him come back and wait awhile.

The light started fading into dusk. Before it grew into complete darkness we rounded a small hillock. He clapped me on the shoulder, pointing ahead through the pines to an encampment of scattered tents in between the trees, pitched in no special pattern with fires here and there glowing in the open. Hurricane lamps flicked a weak light inside several of them giving the place a kind of fairy tale feel. No human beings were in sight, only the darkening dusk and silence.

He led me to a centrally sited tent and pulled back a flap, revealing an empty and cheerless space with one bare camp bed stretcher and a lamp he carefully lit before going.

"I come back – you wait," was all he said and disappeared.

It was not much of a welcome to freedom but I was too tired to worry about it, not an ounce of strength or resistance left in me. I collapsed onto the comfortless stretcher grateful to lie down and take the weight off my feet. I took off my boots and socks feeling the comfort of release from their constriction after three days and miles and miles and miles of marching. They smelled pretty bad, but the relief was sheer heaven.

I lay there, flat on my back, unable to sleep, hands supporting my head as I watched the shadows cast by the flickering lamp play on the roof in a constant display of changing shapes. Something more had to happen. I hadn't endured the last few demanding hours just to lie down and sleep in the bareness of an isolated tent. I hadn't struggled through those endless miles to end up like this, to wait in a tent while some unknown Greek went off to wherever. Where was this bloody British Army Major in his Mission located? Where were the British voices I wanted to hear welcoming me, congratulating me on my survival? I drifted in and out of a dreamy sleep, waking, dozing, conscious of the cold seeping through me. What a miserable, bloody place it was. Floating off again I was startled to hear voices coming closer, out of the heavy black darkness, alerting me back into wakeful life. I sat up waiting, uncertain, cold, thirsty and hungry.

A big voice was calling in English, the accent foreign but recognisable. The tent flap ripped open. I looked up, sitting up, a blond headed guy filled the entrance to my bare tent. His great giant of a body came with it, head ducked to avoid the limited space above him. A bulging .45 automatic hung from his belt. He was a huge presence, his uniform vaguely American. He raised a hand in friendly greeting.

"Hi there buddy!" he said, grinning a warm welcome that seemed to fill the tent. He held out a huge open hand, "Good to see you!" I leapt to my feet an grasped it with both of mine feeling a reassuring warmth that went all the way down to my bare toes. "They got you too – eh?"

I couldn't begin to say how much his arrival meant to me but I managed only a feeble "Hello there. Can you help me get to the British Mission," adding, "I don't know where it is but as a British fighter pilot I am trying to find the local major who runs it?"

It wasn't the kind of response I intended. It was the thought that had been my obsession for the last few days and it just came out without thinking.

"Sure, sure. I heard you were here. Came to see how you were going on. I came to get you. These sons-of-bitches round here dunno a goddam thing! They'll keep you stuck here until their boss man says OK for you to go. He's not around. They're bald arsed scared to move any which way without him. You relax there now I'll fix it. First you must have some chow, something hot to drink then we talk about the journey down to the Mission."

It was OK by me. He left. I waited, feeling confident that out in the dark stillness he was organising things in my interests. He blew in with all the suddenness of his first arrival.

"Right! We're going down the mountain. I've fixed it. If we do it now we should be there in a few hours. Its a hard ride down hill."

His well-intentioned message was a shock. I took the package of American K rations he thoughtfully brought me, and the pannikin of hot water to make a drink.

"Thanks that's very good of you," I said, "I haven't had anything much today in the way of food or drink." He retrieved the square carton of ration food, opened it, extracted the coffee capsule, added sugar, stirred the mixture and handed to me.

"There you go, that'll help." It was only lukewarm but had a beautiful sweet flavour. Hungrily I attacked the rest of the ration food, eating it cold, pocketing the more lasting bits, telling him what had happened, where I'd come from, and the main events of the past three days. He listened well, offering a packet of Lucky Strikes. The food, the drink, a cigarette, did things for me, lifting my flagging spirits. So many goodies at once, enjoying pieces of concentrated chocolate, dragging on the cigarette, sipping the warm coffee to make it last.

"You sure have had a tough time of it." He sympathised, "Just say the word when you're ready and we can start off, OK? I got a donkey out of them for you to ride. It's a wooden saddle. You might have to get used to that!" He was looking to see if I accepted. "They have given us a good guide. He'll take us down. We'll sure need him in the dark."

Too exhausted to protest at any of his suggestions about going on into the night I felt I had to accept.

"Alright," I said, "and by the way, they call me Mac, what about you?"

"OK, Mac" he grinned "My name is Hank," and with that he led me out of the tent into the still darkness outside.

We found two Greeks, smelling of the native tobacco they smoked, rifles slung across their shoulders, and two donkeys waiting patiently. A light drizzle of rain was settling on everything. That was all I needed. The seat stuck on the donkey's back looked secure enough but promised nothing but discomfort. With the Greeks' help we both mounted up, our legs hanging over either side, Hank's almost touching the ground.

Everything under my soft bottom was bone hard and registered with each step the animal took, a rolling side-to-side motion, a movement that found more sensitive spots under me than I wanted to know about.

We cleared the pine forest and the shelter it gave. The drizzle slowly seeped into my clothes. It was cold and would get colder. The warmth of the animal's flanks helped. The ground started downwards the donkey's gait stiffening against it. I could see no more than the animal's bowed head and the Greek guide leading it. Slipping forward against the iron hard wood of the saddle became extremely painful, numbing my crotch. On we went into the damp darkness, there was to be no relief from discomfort in any form, this nights ride was going to be a truly tortuous experience all the way down. I soon lost track of time with no idea how long the ordeal must continue. I tried every possible minor adjustment in my sitting position but nothing made the slightest difference; it only increased the aches and pains. There was no avoiding the abrasive rubbing along the inside of my thighs and along the calf muscles of my dangling legs. I couldn't even feel the bottom half of my sodden body, everything down there was completely dead, completely sore. The drizzle formed a steady stream of liquid running off the top of my head down into my eyes, straight on, under my shirt, all the way through, a cold squelchy feeling that penetrated all the way into the fleecy lining of my flying boots. My toes were no longer attached to my body by any sensation.

That enduring beast under me kept plodding on, one braced step at a time, stiffened against the downward slope of a path I could not see. There was no choice but to accept with absolute faith my guide's ability to find the way ahead and to handle the animal with a thankless foreigner mounted on its back. I hated that animal and all the painful misery he was inflicting on me, my displeasure increasing with every passing minute.

The space over to our right had a feeling of empty blackness. I knew without seeing, that we must be moving across a steep escarpment. Rivulets of water were streaming down across the way we followed, eroding the loose earth and gravel, threatening to undermine the narrow foothold of our path. It was probably more dangerous than flying through intense flak! I pushed the thought from my mind. It was enough to endure the ride, never mind about the danger. Bugger the danger!

The slow journey was unreal, a kind of nightmare of misery and insecurity: enveloping wet blackness, a frightening sense of blind void beyond the mountainside, straddling a dumb beast as it slithered and skidded its way forward. The persistent drizzle was more than just cold; it penetrated to the very core of me, freezing my aching bones. I wondered if our stumbling group might spill disastrously over some kind of blind precipice and disappear forever. At least it would be a way out. On and on we went, suspended in time. The dull ache from the parachute landing throbbed away in my right knee. When was this going to end! I felt angry. Why must I go on enduring this? But on I went into the wet night, falling forward against the wooden pommel of the donkey's saddle. I shouted to the Greek guide, indicating that I'd had enough; I couldn't go on. He stopped the donkey and produced a piece of rope from nowhere, fastened it securely about my waist, half lifting me back against the rear of that brutal saddle, he looped it around and tied me there. It wasn't much of an adjustment but it held my weight clear of the front of the saddle. We moved on. I was fighting against my weakness; gritting my teeth as I sat there, knowing there was no way-out, only onwards and downwards. I knew I could not give in again.

The hours slipped away into a timeless void as I concentrated on staying alive, just being there, getting through this journey, trying to remain upright in my rolling saddle. My senses spun and slowly I slipped away into a bottomless whirlpool.

The next thing I knew was the sound of a voice coming to me, at first vague and distant, but with a familiar ring to it, far off, cloaked in a haze of darkness. It grew in strength. A hand was shaking my shoulder, gently slapping my face. Slowly it reached my wandering mind.

"Mac! Mac!", an anxious sound to it, "Hey, you alright Buddy?"

Realising my head was cradled in his arms I looked into Hank's face, blurry at first, rain water dripping from him onto me. Where was I?

"Hey man, how yer feeling?"

I slowly came to, recovering my mental process, trying to bring it all into focus. I had collapsed with fatigue, fallen forward over the donkey's neck, checking him in his stride. He'd stopped dead in his tracks. The Greek guide had turned around to see me hanging half off the animal and called Hank in alarm. They'd come back, untied the restraining rope and taken me down wondering what had happened, handicapped by the blindness of the dark wet night around us.

I shook my head against the swirling mist in my brain, trying to sit up, feeling wet and watery, taking a couple of real deep breaths. Trying to get a grip.

"Ah! Hank… I'm…eh… OK, mate. What happened?"

He told me about it. A real patient, understanding explanation. They were all concerned for my well-being. Stupidly, I felt a if I'd given in, just like that! What a bloody fool, falling off the donkey. I'd ridden all the way so far. The guides had done it on their feet and carrying rifles. It was not a very British achievement. I felt ashamed of my failure.

"Yes, sure, I'm OK now, really. Sorry about that. Its been a long day, and a long night, I guess."

They all had a hand helping me to my feet, bracing me against the warm side of the animal, lifting me back on to the iron hard wooden saddle. Making sure I was alright.

"OK, Mac, if you're happy we'll go on now. Should be getting near the village soon."

Into the stride of our ride again I felt at a loss without being sure what the loss was about; a helpless unreal feeling. Then slowly, gripping on to my thoughts, I began to relax. Our descent had flattened out. The donkey was moving without that stiffness of gait needed on the mountain slope. Not a big change but enough of a sensation to make it easier sitting, less painful, feeling his swaying, more rhythmical.

In the half light Hank stopped his donkey and waited for me to come up level.

"Hey Mac, how yer goin' now buddy? Some ride eh? Its just ahead of us now. We're gettin' places. That pathway up there, a real switchback son of a bitch. Sure you're OK now?"

"Yes, I'm fine Hank – almost a normal guy again. Thanks."

We rode together the darkness fading around us, lifted by the pale light of a rising sun just visible above the horizon ahead. A new day was with us. The drizzle had stopped some time back but I hadn't noticed. Hanks guide was saturated, his rifle carried in reverse slope. I chuckled inwardly, we were all completely wet through.

The roadway was adequate for the two donkeys, the surface yellowish in colour, raised slightly above the surrounding ground and pock-marked with puddles of water. The donkey picked his way through them. The first of the village houses in view looked good; clean, whitewashed, set apart from one another. Not a sign of any human activity. We passed on.

"Where we going, Hank?" I asked unnecessarily.

"We'll try finding the Major first. He should be around. Probably still asleep." The sleeping village spread out on each side of the road before us, no visible life, not even a barking dog. Our arrival was an anticlimax. We stopped, "Here we are; the Major's place."

I couldn't believe this was really my journey's end. Every part of me registered its own private protest of pain and stiffness. The numbness below my waist was complete and I was sure sensation would never return. Hank shouted two or three times and to my surprise there was little delay. The front door opened to the appearance of an army type.

"Hello, hello!" he called, "good to see you. Come on in! Get down from up there and we'll do something to dry you out. A cup of hot tea should go down well after your long ride here." He addressed me, greeting Hank with a friendly half salute, "Good ride, Hank?"

"What do you think? Hank said, "sure was the wettest I've known. Bloody too long too." Hank and his guide rode on, "I'll see you later, have a good rest," and they went their way.

"Thanks Hank!" I called after them, seeing him wave over his head in acknowledgement.

I suddenly realised I was locked in that saddle, completely unable to get off. The Major saw the difficulty.

"Let me give you a hand down!"

Half lifting, half supporting, he helped me out of that primitive vice. Never did I want to see that animal again! On the ground, my legs gave way under me, two useless stalks of bone and muscle. I grabbed the donkey to steady myself, almost falling into a pool of rainwater and mud, grateful the animal stood patiently still. It was embarrassing. The Greek guide took my arm, lifting it round his shoulder and supporting me towards the house.

"Sorry about this Major. My circulation will be back in a moment. We're not very good at long days and long nights in the RAF. Too bloody soft, always sitting in aeroplanes!" I tried laughing at my own joke.

"This chap is a bloody marvel. He's walked all night leading me down here and now he's supporting me. I don't even know how to thank him for what he's done.

"Worry not," the Major responded, "I'll tell him what you've said and I'll reward him. I'll reward both of them for their part in rescuing you. It's our normal policy here." It all sounded so neat and tidy.

Entering a large central room they sat me down. Turning to the guide I grasped his hand, saying, "Thanks mate – you're a first class bloke. I owe you a lot." He didn't understand my words but he saw my smile and felt the warm grasp of a grateful hand. Then he left and I never saw him again…

The room in my reassuring shelter was sparsely furnished but warm, dry and clean. It made me feel good. Two Greeks came in, tousle-haired, roused from their beds, smiling the kind of welcome I needed. The Major explained that it was their house. He lodged with them and they had a room for me. We could sort out anything else later.

The wife expressed her concern for me, the state of my clothes, my general look of exhaustion. Speaking reasonable English they wanted to know about me and what had passed that day. I didn't know where to start. I wasn't sure I knew where it had all started.

"First, I want to thank you for receiving me here. Am I tired? you ask. No I'm not tired. It's way past that for me. I feel like the walking dead, standing up dead, lying down dead, or to die. But you cannot imagine how marvellous it is to be in your house, safe, sheltered and secure. I've had the longest day of my life, the hardest twenty-four hours I've ever lived. It's like being born again as a human being. I feel I am with friends. I know I have been with friends all the time. The difference is I can speak to you here and you can speak back again. Wonderful."

While I was talking the woman slipped out, brewed some tea and came back to offer me a huge enamel mug full of the steaming liquid and a plate with a thick slice of honeyed bread. They were an indescribable treat. Nothing ever tasted so good as that first cup of hot sweet tea. I told her that. She shrugged modestly, smiling, showing it was nothing, Just good to be helpful, to see how much I enjoyed it.

"The food not good here. Plenty things we cant get." She shook her head. "Major he help us, we like very much in our house." So that's where it came from! Progressing through the story of my experiences I began to droop. It was getting difficult to be coherent, rambling along, skipping bits out. A heavy sleeping feeling creeping through my wet clothes. They were cold now. Suddenly madam stood up.

"You go rest. I fix your clothes. You sleep, wake up, they all dry, ready for you. Put outside room door, I find, take away – OK?"

Her husband led me up a short flight of stairs, "See you later Major. If I ever wake up again!"

"Yes! Sleep well Mac. You deserve it."

The room was clean. Almost empty. A bare floor, one bed against the whitewashed wall, a single pillow, a couple of blankets on top and a single chair with a folded towel. They had put some sort of animal skin on top. A stylish touch. He motioned towards the bed. It was for me. "Here – for you"

"Thank you very much. It looks absolutely marvellous," I waited impatiently for him to go. God be praised it looked like the answer to the sole wish of my life, somewhere to sleep forever and ever! I slipped out of my squelching, fleece-lined flying boots, emptying water onto the clean board floor. They would take some drying out. My socks were sodden and my toes still somewhere beyond the feel of my exhausted body. Shedding the clothes was a real pleasure, stacking them neatly just outside the door. Stripped off to bare skin I felt better. It was the first time since Brindisi. The towel dried me off. That helped even more. Now to relax in safety. I collapsed on to the bed, wriggled down beneath the coarse blankets and the animal skin, surrendering to an overwhelming weakness. My fight against the tormenting of my senses was over. A heavy drowsiness crept up and enveloped me. I thought to pray a moment wanting to thank God for my rescue, for still being there. I had not made it alone, only God could have done that, and I slipped into the peace of sleep, sleep, sleep.

CHAPTER 8

Airlift to Safety

Daylight shafted through the window of my room. I turned over, not wanting to finish what must have been the longest sleep of my life. It was certainly the best I could remember. Something quickly shattered my sleepiness away. It had disturbed me awake. My arms, my whole body, was alive and on edge, nearly driving me mad. I scratched almost everywhere at once, gritting my teeth against a raging kind of sensitivity. I flung the blankets off to look. There, to my horror, were long ugly red welts along the line of veins in my arms. It felt the same around my neck. Streaks of pink torment. I couldn't stop scratching. It made no impression, gave no relief at all. I knew I must control or harm myself.

Outside the door I found my clothes dry and neatly folded, just like she'd promised. I must have slept for about twenty hours but at that moment, still itching, there was no place for more. Dressing helped to distract the feeling of irritation everywhere. I went down the steps not wanting to disturb the house but feeling I wanted to shout out against it.

"Bed bugs, old boy," the Major was instantly informative. Sympathetic but not unduly so. Too casual about my discomfort, "nothing much we can do about it I'm afraid. Got some bug powder which you can have. They are certainly voracious little buggers, seem to gorge all night," and he chuckled to lessen the situation. "You sit down, have a cup of coffee. You'll feel better for it. Have a good sleep?" Then he remembered, "apart from the bed bugs?" We'll go off, have a look see around the place. Not much here really, just a small village, bit primitive. All we can safely hold for the moment. If the Hun comes at us we can scoot for the mountains. Not much chance of that as they are gradually pulling out around these parts."

He droned on, fixing my coffee while I squirmed and twitched against my itching. It helped. The worst seemed to be easing off. "I'd like you to have a look at our landing strip – give it the expert eye – professional point of view, eh? We're expecting a Dakota to fly in at night when all is ready. It'll be the plane to take you out with the Americans. They're going back to base. You'll go with them." he chattered on, talking away, not waiting or wanting an answer. Maybe he hadn't had a good chance to talk at anyone for some time. A

The Author, somewhat bedraggled after being shot down, 1944.

friendly chap, all smiles and military moustache. "You`ve timed it well. That plane I mean".

"I've got to make a call first off, want to see our radio operator, get him to let Cairo know you are in our hands, make sure the Dakota has space, things like that. I'll be back for you in about half an hour. OK?" and off he went leaving me to that big mug of black coffee, sweet and delicious.

The two Greek owners of the house were nowhere to be seen. Maybe out in the fields? I got to thinking how it would be for my folks to learn I'd gone down. Fiji was a remote world away. I knew how mother and father worried that their only son would be lost to this world. Father was a wartime colonel. He knew these things happened but they both still fretted. It was always painful for those at home. Several next of kin had written to the squadron at times, sending copies of the official signals and correspondence, pleading for more personal details as though the words received were not enough. "Regret to inform you your son is reported missing but believed uninjured as the result of air operations stop. Enquiries are being made through the international Red Cross Committee and any further information received will be communicated to you immediately stop Should news of him reach you from any other source please advise this department stop Letter follows shortly stop No information is to be given to the Press stop."

The bureaucrats charged with sending out these signals were coldly efficient with the emphasis on coldly. They processed missing people by the hundreds without doing more than operate the mechanics of the process. They were not callous because they could not know more from distant London than the name, number and rank of each individual subject. Even on the squadron we protected ourselves from being hurt when one of us was lost. We were not cynical about it only real, cushioning emotions against the pain of it because of its frequency. It was a different story at the receiving end. Mums and Dads, wives, sons and daughters and all the others were consumed with aching pain. To them it was very real and very personal, very tragic.

The Air Ministry follow-up letters were little better, detailing the event in the belief that a next of kin would be comforted...

"The telegraphic report from Air Force Headquarters, North Africa, states that the Mustang aircraft in which your son was flying was hit by enemy fire approximately 45 miles north west of Salonika.

If he is a prisoner of war he should be able to communicate with you in due course. Meanwhile enquiries are being made through the international Red Cross Committee, and as soon as any definite news is received you will be at once informed..."

Followed by the same pattern of caution regarding the Press and hearing from any other source, explaining this, saying "in order to avoid prejudicing his chance of escape by undue publicity, should he still be at large in enemy occupied territory." Then the pious commiseration – "The Air Council desire me to express their sympathy with you in your present anxiety." Signing off, declaring the signatory to be 'Your obedient Servant.'

Obedient! We understood well and sympathetically why next of kin in distant countries wrote pleading letters for personal details. How they felt with the jargon of official messages. Who was the Air Council anyway expressing heart felt sympathy. Often the follow up was even more confusing. Well! I thought, I'd seen it all with others – now it was me.

I heard the Major coming long before he entered the house again. The village was quiet without the sounds one might expect, dogs, children, the noises of people in a village.

"There you are," he called dumping a mysterious container on the table. "The bug powder I mentioned. It will do the trick, help you defeat those little buggers."

"Thanks Major. Very good of you. When do you suggest I use it?" "Sprinkle a bit around the blankets and your body where you've got bites."

"What about now," acknowledging his words of wisdom wanting anything to help rid me from the itching. I grabbed it, dashed up stairs took off my clothes and slapped it everywhere in haste, around my testicles, my arms, under my armpits, around my neck. That should do it. I dressed again and joined him "Right. We'll go off and have a recce of the place, look over the strip, familiarise you with the place generally. Like to do that?"

I took a good look as he stood talking. Strange in a way to find anyone like him, so typically British, in a remote place like this. Then, of course, it was strange to find myself in a place like this. Yes, he was the type: outwardly quiet ordinarily, normal and reserved, a calm sort of chap without pretensions but tough fibre all the way through, real English, smarter than one might expect here, well turned out, up-brushed military tash, neatly trimmed, cap firmly planted, none of the rakish angle stuff flaunted by RAF types.

"Sounds a good idea to me, Major. By the way, that chap Hank, American. Who are they? What was he doing here?"

Ah! Yes bit of a surprise for you was he? He didn't tell you? They are usually voluble enough. Very friendly and very co-operative. He belongs to our counterparts here, the British Raiding Support Regiment chaps. The Americans are the Rangers. First class fighting material.

They're going for a spell of civilisation again. Not sure we'll get them back. Things are changing fast here now. That was my meaning when I said you were spot on with your timing." He grunted jokingly, "then I don't think you'd accept being shot down would qualify for good timing under any circumstances!"

"You're dead right about that, Major. Not the most enjoyable experience I can assure you!"

We walked on for a while in silence, crossing a stream running through the centre of the village. A pretty picture book setting.

"How are the bug bites now?" he asked, as if he'd just remembered?" I rolled back a sleeve showing the welts. "Yes, nasty. That powder will help. You know it's said they don't go for everybody. Supposed to be very choosy about blood. You're probably a healthy chap, eat plenty of good food – you Air Force chaps always do pretty well!" I couldn't take offence at his humour; his chitchat coming in bursts.

"This way, the strip we're building is clear of the town but still close enough for a quick getaway into the hills. That house over there," he pointed to our left, a small single storey parked over the stream, "that's where we've got our radio operator housed. Andreas, half Greek/ Egyptian, calls up Cairo every night at eighteen hundred. Its done with Morse code, decoded and encoded by him, for me in about half an hour. He'll be the chap to receive the message you want to hear, when the Dakota's coming. Keep close to him!" He smiled at his little joke.

We walked over the rough grass strip, its flatness just reasonable, little hummocks here and there. About a thousand yards long, I thought, maybe fifty yards wide, across the throat of the foothills, a hazard in the dark. He'd have to make his approach in a left hand circuit coming in from the plain – isn't that where the Huns were supposed to be? I was not impressed, thinking to be guarded in my comments. Above all else I wanted that plane to land and take me out, never mind about the Americans. For all I knew, it might be well within the bush pilot competence of the Dakota boys but it looked to me like a death-trap for landing in the dark.

The Major and Greek Partisans – 1944.

"At night," the Major said, prompting my silence, "we've asked for thirty minutes after he flashes us the identity signal for clearance – to light the fires". He pointed out the piles of brushwood lining one side of the strip at fifty-yard intervals, terminating across the far end. "Well? What's your opinion, as a pilot?

I hesitated. They wanted to believe a plane could come in under complete darkness with only brushwood fires indicating the limits and then safely go out again? Well! God bless them! And those hills? Then the fires across one end only? Maybe there never was a wind change in these parts.

"Major, are you trying to tell me a pilot is expected to come in the dark of night, using his landing lights only, and land on that strip in one whole piece!" I clamped shut. Opening my big mouth was a mistake. They didn't know about these things. Was I delaying my chances of getting out of here? The landing looked difficult enough for broad daylight, with everything clearly visible, but under the cover of darkness?

"Its difficult for me to give you a real opinion." I blustered, "Mustangs have a much higher landing speed than Dakotas, takes longer to bring them to a halt. Dakotas float in. Once they get the tail wheel down – no problem. All I can say is – if it has been made to their specification then it must be OK. Let's hope we soon find out. Presumably the Germans will react to something like this – how long for them to get here?"

"We have done exactly as they asked and received their OK. But you think it's not long enough?" He sounded to counter any doubts. I shook my head, shrugged my shoulders, spread my hands in surrender. I really didn't know. I knew I couldn't land a plane on it, but I'd said too much already.

"If its all to their specification, Major, then it's OK!"

"You asked about the Hun out there..." he gestured in the direction of the open plain. "We'll do what we can, place a screening patrol as far out as possible. They'll give us all the warning we need."

'That's it then,' I thought. The Dakota was my passport back to the squadron, the last thing I wanted to do was interfere with that.

The sun was warming me, perspiration appearing on my forehead. I began to itch again.

"Would you mind if I pay a call on Andreas, major? Have a look at his set up."

"Not at all, old boy. I'll leave you to it. Got some business in the village with the head man."

He went off. I made for the little house on the stream, aware that where I'd spread the bug powder was getting more and more sensitive. Before I'd made it there I was walking with my legs apart like a bull with oversized testicles. It was sore!

Andreas came out, greeting me like an old friend. He was a fine looking young man a welcoming smile across his face. He waited for me to speak first. "Hello Andreas. The Major gave you the details about my bailing out and rescue? Good! That'll get through to my squadron and next of kin. They'll know I am still alive". Not standing on ceremony in my urgency, I continued, "But at the moment you could help in another way. I spread a lot of bug powder around my balls and under my armpits. It's getting a bit painful, nearly driving me mad."

"Yes," he said, "I know when I use it first time. It happens to me. Best you wash it. I get you some water, a towel."

It was a primitive stone floor bathroom but more than enough to strip off and wash everywhere. My penis and testicles were red and raw. I couldn't see my arse but it felt the same. My arms were an angry pink.

I dried and dressed, thankful for his assistance. Having a piss revealed the lavatory to be a small square hole in concrete, two-foot prints either side, for positioning, the village stream gurgling away below it. I wondered what might be down stream from here, fast running water or not!

He was a chatty fellow, telling me about the local set up, how the British arranged their messing, the cost of living, things like that.

"No one have money, only Major have gold sovereigns, local peoples have only okas of wheat for buying. One shop in village, nothing. If you want buy something he want okas of wheat." His message loud and clear, I did want something. All my personal property was on my back and feet. Not one other item of encumbrance did I possess but desperately I needed a toothbrush. 'Yes' I might get one in the shop. First I needed some of the Major's treasure chest. A thought struck me.

"Andreas, have you got a spare room, a bed here. You said you get rations for here?"

"Sure" he had my message straight off. I would be welcome to share with him. He looked pleased about it, a guest of honour, no less. The Major hesitated, a little uncertain.

"I think I'll get on well with Andreas, a very pleasant young man and my food can be added to his conveniently. He assured me there would be no extra costs. The house is a rented as one and", I added with emphasis, "his place is free of bed bugs. That suits me a thousand per cent, Major!" It was all settled. Even the toothbrush charged to his account with the little store. Andreas telling me "it costs three okas of wheat."

I sauntered to the far end of the village curious to meet the R.S.R. chaps. They were a swashbuckling group of friendly young, unconventional, army types. Interested to hear my story saying the lack of attention from the Greeks higher up the mountain could be expected,

"That bunch of bloody commies, ELAS are all for consolidating their own position, waiting to take power after the Germans leave. They'll accept all we have to give and keep it ready for that day. They have no respect for us, only for what our air drops bring them."

Joining the R.S.R. again after my first meal with Andreas was the most enjoyable time since being shot down. We gathered around their open-air fire, exchanging experiences, contributing songs, forgetting the horrors of war. Fiji was a talking point before I went off to bed early.

The days of waiting passed by, all clear blue skies and fretting boredom. Nothing to do, nowhere to go, wandering here and there within my prescribed boundaries, restless and empty, longing to fly again. I'd forgotten, the stimulus of operations was like a drug to my system. I needed to do it. My inaction was demoralising. I belonged to no one and no one wanted me. Everybody around always had a warm greeting, a few words, nothing else. My only achievement was an improvement in accuracy with that small square hole and its two guiding footprints in the concrete slab, listening to the flow of bubbling water under my bare bottomed crouch. I knew a surprise one morning, hearing the Major call my name.

"Mac, you there, Mac"? Showing pleasure in seeing me again after what was, in fact, a meeting in the village only two hours ago. No preamble he sailed right in, " I would like you to represent the British point of view at a local political rally tomorrow morning. Say something for Churchill; they admire him. They have these gatherings quite often and I've run out of anything new for them!" If he'd struck in the face I couldn't have been more startled. What an alarming idea, I couldn't do anything like that! Stand up in front of a bunch of Greeks, not speaking a word of their language, and tell them about something almost as foreign to me as it was to them!

"Major! You've got to be joking. I haven't a clue about things like that! What in hell do I know about Churchill, leave alone their lives and their wishes?"

He placed a cajoling hand on my shoulder, an intimate touch of encouragement against my protest.

"Come on, old boy. It's not as bad as that. It'll do a lot for our position here. They know all about you being shot down fighting for their cause against the Hun. News spreads like wildfire in this place. They'll be alive with curiosity about you." He followed with flattery, "Not many fighter boys around, you know. What about it? I would deem it a personal favour. It doesn't matter much what you say to them. Andreas will translate as you go along. He's good at it"

I was a pushover. How could I resist his approach; part flattery, part appealing to bravado and my sense of duty? I owed him so much. I owed them all so much and more importantly, I still had to get out of this place with their help.

"OK, Major. I'll do it – but let me tell you, I'm scared as hell by the idea and God knows what I will say!"

They were all crowded into what appeared the schoolhouse, jabbering away to one another, the hot and sticky atmosphere smelling strongly of tobacco. Andreas beckoned me up on to the platform. The noise stopped to look me over. I sat at the centre table feeling naked, a hollow in my midriff. I had to endure two speakers haranguing the hot room packed with silent and attentive men. No women in sight. It was undoubtedly a political meeting going on and I wondered why I was there at all; their words were incomprehensible, boring, my seat solid hard wood, no back rest. I felt more and more heavy-lidded, waiting for my turn to come. The chap on his feet shouting the odds, waving his arms round like a semaphore signaller, paused, half turned towards me, breaking my cow-stare coma. Andreas stage whispered,

"It for you, speak now. He tell them you British flying man. How you shoot German planes. How you come this place."

Slowly I rose to my feet, uncertain, thoughtful. I'd rehearsed something for several hours but it had left me. The faces down there all focussed, expectancy written on each, waiting. I walked around the table, stealing time, almost knocking it over in my clumsiness, exposed, unqualified, incompetent.

"Say something for England to the fighting people of Greece, for Winston Churchill," the Major prompted. I stood before them, trying hard to recollect what I'd worked out.

They waited, sitting quietly. Someone clapped and the hot smelly room burst into welcoming applause. I hadn't opened my mouth! Taking a couple of deep breaths I launched into it.

"You are my brother fighters, comrades. You give me a great honour today asking me to talk to you about the war we have been fighting against the Germans for many years now. I am only one fighter pilot, flying aeroplanes in the Royal Air Force. My Job to destroy the Luftwaffe's planes and their trains, their motor transport, anything that will defeat them." Flushed, excited, I was carried away in my own fluency of words. I had completely forgotten they needed Andreas's translation. I stopped, embarrassed, turning towards him apologetically, signalling it was his turn.

He seemed to go on far longer than I'd expected, watching them, faces raised in rapt attention, nodding acceptance.

"My nation of peoples, the British, is strong. We have fought the war for many years in many places to give peoples like you their freedom. Freedom to think and to act as God wants them to think and live." Andreas made the points in their language.

"My King and Mr Churchill support all the races and peoples of the world who believe in the rights of freedom for everyone. Not only freedom from war but freedom to eat and to sleep as free men and women and I hope this will be for Greece."

Another translation pause, wondering how I was doing. They looked to still be interested and patient, waiting to get my messages in their language.

"The Greek nation of the future, in the years to come, for each one of you, for your children and for their children is in your own hands." I wondered if Andreas might be thinking it was enough. With the pauses added in I seem to have been holding forth too long. I went on.

Greek villagers gathering to hear my words of wisdom, 1944.

"The Greek nation has a history of democracy going back many hundreds of years. Your ancestors were the people who invented democracy and this war has been a fight to preserve that precious state of living. The Nazis have tried to destroy it and now they are almost beaten…"

Just one more burst, I thought.

"You have guns now – everybody has guns now – but the future we must all seek can not be gained with guns only with votes, votes for democracy and freedom. Thank you all for inviting me here and thank you all for listening to me. Let us go forward to finish this terrible war, then we can stop killing one another, find peace and enjoy our lives as God intended."

I exhaled an enormous sigh. It was over, thank goodness! I thought I had done it well enough for them, said what was asked of me properly, leaving them the message about not killing one another after we had all pulled out of their country – a vain hope!

Andreas put what I had said into his concluding translation, looked at me and nodded, signalling, 'that's it'.

Almost before he had spoken the last few words they began shouting their approval, raising excited fists, pumping the air, voicing some slogan I could not understand. It was wild, approving applause. An embarrassed warmth crept up my neck into my cheeks. Elated with my reception, covering my feelings, I went down from the platform and out of the heat of the meeting room. Murmurs of approval and tentative pats on the back followed me. The best day I'd had so far.

I shared the evening meal with the army chaps, enjoying their light hearted banter aimed at the ELAS meeting, gibes about 'boys in blue' and the luck of a colonial in waiting to go back to the relative comfort of war torn civilisation in Italy. Grouped around their outside fire we swapped stories about home and its remoteness from this place. The food we might enjoy once again when it was all over, the women waiting for our favours. With the Hun on the run from these parts, the exciting allied advances in Europe, it could not be long now. Hitler must throw in the towel soon. Our optimism was subjective. We had had enough; time was now to stop it before all the years of our young lives were spent.

At transmission time each night I sat with Andreas, fascinated, listening in anticipated suspense to his exchanges with an unseen operator miles away in Cairo. The flurry of dots and dashes coming in were a mystery until his click-clickety response said 'end of transmission' and he decoded the grouped letters letting me read before taking them to the Major.

Each night I read the messages, yearning to learn the Dakota would be with us, each night a disappointment, then, finally, it came in.

"This it, this the one!" Andreas smiled in his pleasure at telling me what I wanted so desperately to hear. "It for tomorrow night. The fly-in." As if I didn't know what he was on about. I'd caught a sense of joy before he'd tapped out the shut down code. Yet I had no way of knowing what was in those last groups he'd written in response to the di-da-di-da-di-da-dit in his earphones.

I grasped his hand in both of mine shaking violently, wanting to show my joy, express my feelings physically.

"That's bloody marvellous, Andreas! You're a clever man!" He switched everything out and we left together, crossing back over the stream, he to tell the Major, me to let the RSR and Ranger boys know. The good news was for all of them, not just those who would be flying out. The Dakota would bring in a load of goodies for those who were to stay behind.

The day was long in going. I walked about the place not knowing what to do with myself, impatiently wasting the hours, waiting for darkness to fall, chuckling to myself. No preparation was required: apart from my acquired toothbrush and, subsequently, a comb, all I had was the brown battle dress trousers, army type shirt and battle dress jacket I stood up in. My fleece lined flying boots had never completely dried out, even though each night I'd taken out the soles, opened them up hoping the heat from our cooking fire would penetrate.

The darkness wrapped around us had a crystal clear, magic, feel to it. A canopy of big bright stars stretched from the horizon on one side, reaching out over the plain, to the ridge of mountains just visible in the moonlight. It had a dream like quality. Each spot of twinkling light overhead seemed to acknowledge my prayers. The moon was bright and just rising. It was a perfect night for a blind landing.

Of course, the same favourable conditions also applied to the Germans out there, wherever they may be. How far away, I wondered? But I had no intention of putting that question to anybody. We had assembled with a full muster of Raiding Support Regiment and American Ranger chaps, plus a force of ELAS partisans spread out along the full length of our landing ground. Were they here out of curiosity or here to defend? 'Leave it, leave it,' I thought, 'stay with the all-important issue of the night.'

I moved along the small pilot fires scattered down one side at regular intervals, seeing the circles of armed guerrillas sitting roasting corncobs in the glowing embers. The smell was delicious. They talked quietly, enlivened every now and again with rumbles of carefree laughter. Seeing Andreas in one group I stopped, inviting myself into their circle. He introduced me indicating each one with expressive hands, in the way of the Greeks. 'They ask if you like to go back to Italy tonight? If you have family there'? Polite, interested questions.

"No Andreas, tell them I have no family. Only my fighter squadron. They are my war family. I want to be with them again."

A burly man, heavily moustached, raked his cob of corn from the fringe of coals, skewered and offered it. Though it was too hot to hold I spoke the Greek words for thank you, learned from Andreas during my passing stay. I heard grunts of approval. The charred kernels had a delicious sweet flavour, but were tough to bite and tough to chew; a welcome distraction to suppress my excitement.

As time went on the conversation died. We sat in mutual silence. A thin dew dampened my clothes and the ground around us. I was beginning to feel the drop in temperature. It was nothing. My spirits were impervious to any type of distraction. It was after midnight. I could almost hear the silence. Some of the Greeks in our circle spread themselves, dozing off. All was quiet.

A change slowly spread within our circle, gathering by the second, a stirring among us. Their acute hearing had detected the sound of a distant aircraft engine, at first an uncertain faint buzz but growing more distinct, slowly but surely. I heard it as they started calling attention between themselves, my ears were alerted by their reactions. I fastened onto it. Andreas called to me, "You hear airplane noise?"

I had no need to answer him, it was unmistakable, a thrumming beat very different from the sound of the Luftwaffe twin engines, for sure. It had to be our Dakota.

The whole place came to life, tense, excited, chattering without wanting an answer, heads uplifted searching the night sky, watching to see if any of the stars were blanked out. The noise was clear now, a beautiful throbbing sound, engine throttled back. But where was that plane above us? All eyes wide open, we scanned for it, looking for the flash of an Aldis lamp.

Then I saw it, low down to the south of us, winking a coded identity signal in dots and dashes. It had to be for us. The sight stirred our group into a frenzied expectation.

"This is it, this is it!" shouted Andreas for my benefit. He lifted his own Aldis and click/clacked the ground response they would be looking for. He got the OK back. The shouting travelled along the strip, gaining in sound as it went 'Light the fires, light the fires!' Urging everyone into action wanting to make sure they would be ready in time. There was no second chance if we bungled it.

The excited interplay between ground and air, through the winking Aldis lamps, asking, answering, saying in its final message of green light, 'OK all clear – safe to go ahead with our landing', stirred our waiting body of men into willing action. They rushed to each pile of dormant brushwood eagerly torching it into a fiery life. The careful preparations ensured the flames took hold quickly, but not quick enough for my liking. The Dakota circled for minutes that seemed like hours waiting for our primitive beacons to indicate a safe way in. I wanted to shout "Here we are, welcome, come down to us – please, don't go away!"

We jumped around like groups of schoolboys, hoping nothing would prevent success. I knew the green light signal from the plane meant, 'I can see the fires lighting up for my landing, I respond to your urging, I wont go away, I'll come in and land,' yet I knew he still had to safely touch down and stop before I could go back. Before my wild wanderings were over, before my tired waiting was ended. It needed only a safe landing.

The bonfires were stoked into bright flame, a glorious sight, their crackling audible above the engine noise, a dancing pattern of light cast by the flames against the blackness around us. Were they bright enough for the pilot to see from his cockpit? Would they lead him along a glide path to touch down? Could he halt the plane in a safe distance from the end row of flames? All the possibilities of fault rolled around me waiting and praying.

For something to do I went looking for the Major, calling his name in the intermittent light of the beacon fires. He was standing apart from a group of excited men, outwardly calm, looking to see where the Dakota circled above. Wanting something to say I called his attention, "Hello, Major, bloody marvellous isn't it. The plane at last? What happens, by the way, if the Germans are on their way towards us right now? We're pretty vulnerable, aren't we?" feeling it was a foolish question.

He turned, with a look that confirmed it was a stupid question, casually answering as if it was only an ordinary problem anyway.

"No need to worry about that, old boy. The lads are out there. They'll look after us. Anyway, you'll hear the gunfire long before anyone gets too close. Worry not, worry not! You'll be out of here tonight, safe and sound again back in Italy."

His censure quietened me down, calmed all my wild anxieties. He knew about these things and had faith in the few chaps ordered to look after our wider perimeter, some of those good-humoured swashbuckling pongoes I'd met in this lonely outpost.

"Yes, thanks Major. If I don't see you again before I go I want you to know how much I appreciate all you've done while I've been here. Thanks, more especially for my return to safety. That's a debt I can never repay." I left it at that, embarrassed.

The flames slowly increased, crackling louder, shooting sparks into the darker overhead canopy. It was enough for them.

The engine noise swept out and away from us making a circuit pattern, his landing lights forking into the darkness, feeling for a way into an approach line with the strip. I heard him throttle down. There was no wind to test his approach. It looked as it should do. He lined up on the fires, slowly losing height, judging the distance to first point of touch down in the uncompromising dark. I held my breath, listening to hear if he'd open up throttles and go round again after a missed landing. It wasn't going to be easy. Lower and lower, his lights lost height. Through the last few feet I knew he was committed. He bounced on the rough surface of the strip, careered into the air again, bounced a second time and stuck. The plane swept past us at breakneck speed, engines idling, all dust, noise and confusion as he swept to a stop at the far end. It had been a close run thing. He had swung the plane to avoid the line of flaming beacons. A safe landing and a marvellous bloody effort of airmanship!

Thank God! I rushed after him. Seeing the glint of the two whirling propeller blades reflecting the red shimmer of bonfire flames. The engine noise slowly died off and ground to dead silence. He'd stopped, deciding he'd stay there. The whole experience of arrival, identification, friend or foe, the approach, touch down and landing was complete, a joyous success. I dashed up to the long sloping shape waiting for the doors to swing open, crackling flames and shouting figures all around venting their pleasure at this intrusion. No one anywhere in the world was more welcomed. The doors went back against the fuselage and two crew members appeared in the opening, possibly wondering at the moving mob of bodies and the pyrotechnic glow below them.

"Hello there", I shouted, "what a magnificent landing. Welcome." They lowered the stepladder making contact with the ground, responding to us, probably more relieved than anybody at making it in safely.

Without any apparent orders or specific direction, the partisans formed into a disciplined human chain waiting to unload the crates from inside the plane, as if to some predetermined plan.

I wasn't quite sure what I wanted to do next. Only to climb in, up the flimsy ladder, get inside and wait there until we started up and took off again. But other things had to be done. I stood aside looking and seeing and wondering at the willingness around me to help unload.

Each crate coming out received willing hands to be manoeuvred away to the side of the strip clear of the flaming bonfires. It seemed to take hours before the loadmaster called "OK, that's the last one. Where are the returning passengers? You can climb aboard now. Inside."

The American Rangers clambered up with practised ease and disappeared into the black hole interior. I went to go, hesitated a moment, searching the heads around, wanting to find the Major and Andreas, wanting to say a last good bye to my two main links with sanity over the fortnight I'd lived in the place. They'd disappeared into the night, never to be seen by me again. Sad in a way. I did want to share something of my pleasure.

Scrambling in, holding down my excitement, I stumbled into the cold metal cavern of the rescue machine. The chattering Americans were there in sound but not in clear sight. They made a welcome space for the British fighter pilot in their midst.

"Here buddy, take this one near me. Here's the seat belt." It was Hank. I hadn't seen him since that nightmare journey on the back of our donkeys in the rain.

"How yer doing Hank? This is the life, eh? Better than riding an old moke in the cold rain on a mountainside!"

"Hell!" he said above the noise around us, "that was one tough journey." Yes, indeed, I thought, coming from a battle hardened Ranger was clear endorsement of the worst endurance test I ever knew. We filled the plane with the sound of the pleasure we felt at going back to civilisation, the laughing noise floated around me. The overhead light winked its starting up warning message, the engines turned over in sequence, spluttering and coughing into sustained life. He test roared each to power and without hesitation swung the plane facing down the strip and opened up to full power. The hollow drumming in my ears altered as the Dak's tail came up to flying attitude. She bounced once, twice, lightened and lifted into the air. We were off, flying en route for Italy, ears popping, gaining altitude, out over German-held territory. The noise level and the vibration prevented anything but shouting-into-ear conversation. Hank handed me a welcome Lucky Strike, lit it and smiled his pleasure. A soothing drag did a lot for me. I sat huddled, uncomfortably cold, as we gained height, closing my eyes to sleep away the hours of flying before us, not succeeding.

Undoing my seat harness belt I stumbled and tripped my way to the cockpit, tapped the pilot on the shoulder, smiled a greeting and motioned a friendly 'hello'. The noise level was better up here, ahead of the engines perfectly synchronised to a constant hum of power. He lifted off his helmet and presented his ear.

"Marvellous landing, that. I congratulate you."

He nodded, accepting the compliment. "Bit tough judging the last couple of hundred feet. The bonfires were distracting. Wasn't too sure of the surface. Thought I might have to go around again and make a flatter approach. It worked! You a flyer?"

"Yes, Mustangs – 249 Squadron".

Each time we spoke the other proffered an ear, working like a couple of puppets.

"Shot down about two weeks ago strafing Focke Wolf 190s on a Salonika air strip. Bloody hairy business. Baled out. The partisans rescued me – been here until you arrived tonight. You were the best thing I'd seen – forever!"

His broad grin acknowledged my story, making a face of sympathy. He was looking out ahead, through the windscreen into black featureless space waiting for time and distance to pass. I thought, 'Not for me. What a dull job they have, thank God its theirs and not mine! The instrument panel covered in luminous dials looked reassuring, everything appeared to be working OK. I stood there for a while longer, nothing more to say.

"Ok, I'll go back," I thumbed in the direction over my shoulder. "Thanks for the ride. First class. I'll do the same for you any day!" He half saluted and I returned to my cold metal bucket to sit and dream.

I felt I must be about the luckiest chap alive to have come out of that. My parents would receive another signal confirming I was still of this world. Mother would be thrilled, offer prayers of thanksgiving and prayers of hope that I would survive the remaining time of the war.

We landed at first light of day, a real bumpy one with a stiff cross wind. He taxied his plane to its dispersal and shut the engines down. The doors opened and the Rangers transport was there to take them off. The crew climbed down and walked away, leaving me to my own devices. A couple of airman chocked and secured the plane. I had no idea what came next. I didn't belong to anyone or anything. It was another anti-climax. There was no one to ask and no one to meet me.

CHAPTER 9

Back to the War

"Can you tell me where I would find the Air Movements office, airman?" I asked.

"Yes, Sir," he responded, pointing to a group of huts about two hundred yards away. "Should be somebody there on duty."

"Thanks" I said and wandered off, looking very much like a tramp: dirty, probably smelly and very unkempt. I so much wanted to feel at home again with 249. This was a bitter disappointment, hard to accept in my tired and hungry state.

The duty corporal listened to my story, uncertain about accepting it at face value. He didn't risk saying 'I don't believe you, or how you say you got here' he just took the best way out by ringing his superior.

"I've got an officer here, Sir, says he just came in on a Dakota from Greece – shot down about two weeks ago and rescued by the partisans." He listened to the response. "Yes, Sir. Yes, Sir." He put the receiver down and turned to me. "The duty officer says remain here until he arrives."

A bit curt, I thought, but I just said, "OK". Hopefully I might be getting somewhere. I certainly wasn't expecting to be greeted like a hero after losing a brand new Mustang, but I did want to see familiar faces again, to feel welcomed, get some sympathy after all I had endured, but there was no personal contact of any shape or form, the machine would have to process me.

The duty officer was more reassuring, taking me to the special unit set up to process vagabonds of war like myself. It proved to be in good hard and impersonal working over. I was stripped down first to nothing at all, told to discard every possession (every possession?) naked as the day I was born.

"What are you going to do with those? They are the only clothes I have?" I said.

"Burn them, Sir. You'll receive a completely new kit. We leave you with your two meal tickets – nothing else." Oh well! They were in a state anyway. Next came the debugging. If the Grecian bed bugs had laid eggs up my orifice they would not be safe! The dehumanising process pumped debugging powder into my every nook and cranny. I moved on to the comparative luxury of a warm shower, a thorough scrub down, like a sheep going through a dip. Dried and clean I was presented for a completely new outfitting, top to bottom – boots and all – in best army brown. They said not to dress before the medical officer gave me a thorough going over. He showed special interest in my scarlet balls and penis.

"My God that must have been very strong bug powder, but you'll be fine. You can put our clothes on now. The corporal will take you on to Administration."

They had made me a clean human being again – now I had to be correctly processed, name, meal tickets inspection, a new pay book, a new Form 1250 Identification and some money. The debriefing was thorough and patiently received. When I came to the bit about ELAS holding back, receiving supplies and weapons, preparing for the internal struggle to come it went down in detail, almost with a conspiratorial whisper.

I felt restored. Clean, hygienic, newly dressed, a person again with money and access to more through my new paybook. Taking the notes he passed over I thought of that treasure chest the Major kept in his room full of gold sovereigns. I could have pinched some!

"We will arrange for your transport to the rest camp at Sorrento. You have a full fortnight's recuperation leave". Recuperation? I thought. Recuperating from what? I'd been sitting on my arse like a spare thing at a wedding for nearly two weeks. Recuperation? My request to go straight back on to the Squadron fell on stony ground.

"Sorry, old chap, that's how it is."

He was following what the machine of war directed. "I'm sure you'll enjoy it, a lovely setting and specially organised to refresh anyone who goes there for a rest. You know, people like yourself who've been through a pretty dramatic experience, aren't necessarily a good judge of what is best for them. Go off and enjoy yourself there. I'd swap places with you. By the way, you know you will be able to contact your squadron from there."

He was only trying to be kindly.

It was a waste of time knocking it, I had to go anyway, but the romantic location of the rest camp, perched high above the cliffs at Sorrento, with the sweeping Bay of Naples below, its surface like blue glass and the isle of Capri beyond, was completely wasted on me. I was demoralised, grumpy and against the world. I hadn't come all this way into the war to loaf or laze along the cliffs, or climb down the precipitous steps to swim in the sea. It was not for me, and I suffered more miserable boredom, wondering what to do to pass the time until the next meal.

In the first week I rang the squadron, the only family I knew, where I could expect warmth, comforting sympathy, and tried to arrange for my premature release from this beautiful prison of Sorrento. They were pleased to hear from me again, to learn I was safely back. How was I? What had happened? Best leave it until I could give a full account. But when it came to my plea for rescue from dreary boredom they said 'no dice'. It was not allowed. Take the rest to the full, silly man. Enjoy it. Surely paradise compared to base camp. We talked on a bit about what had happened, what was happening on the squadron but all the time there was no pushing aside the machine, no coming to fetch me: "Sorry, not on, old boy."

It helped to be in touch, to know they still wanted me when the situation allowed. I relaxed a little, comforted to know that my family unit was still there. My tension eased. I started feeling human again.

At the rest camp there was plenty of companionship to be had. Others had experiences to share, different times, different places, different tensions and different approaches to their problems. Some were in a high old state of nerves and trying to settle down, mocking the war, its purpose and their place in it. What was it all about anyway? What was going to happen when they went home? Not long now.

All this futile bloody fighting. What for? They brought out my sense of unquestioning loyalty.

"That is what you signed up for. Fighting for King and country, mate!" I said.

"Balls!" one replied, "You've been brainwashed!"

I couldn't go with that. Bloody pongoes!

But I began to get the feel of the place, adjusting like they all said I would, until the day came when a call summoned me to the medic's office. He knocked me for a six, announcing, "It's your lucky day. Your transport from 249 is here! He was down this way collecting urgent spares from the depot and was told to look in on chance. It's a couple of days early but I'm happy enough to release you. How about that? You're in good shape now. Almost sane again!"

It was bloody marvellous, yet in a perverse kind of way I wasn't sure now about losing those two days of peace and beauty. It took less than a quarter of an hour to collect up my few possessions, sign out and climb aboard the truck. The driver, taken aback by my exuberance, happy to be alive, excited about going home again, played it low – "Yes, sir, yes sir," he muttered, uncommitted.

The long drive was nothing. Sitting there in silence, pleased with myself, I wondered about getting back on ops again.

We arrived in the late evening. It was a joy. I saw the new tin hut Officers Mess

"The first one burnt down," the driver told me, "too much hundred-octane fuel through the feed pipe into our makeshift stove. The forty-gallon drum exploded, back flashed to the overload tank outside. Lovely sight, but could have been very nasty indeed. We lost the furniture and the bar and most of the bottles in it. Very sad stuff! Our new modification is OK. Safe enough now! 'We'll need it. The winds up here have been bloody freezing!"

A group of the other pilots emerged from the Mess coming forward to greet me, each wanting to shake my hand, offering the warmth of personal contact. I had missed their companionship so much.

Keeping pace with their interest in my survival was overwhelming. The hands thrust at me, their faces expressing pleasure, questions coming like a machine gun, first this one, then that one, slapping my back "Good to see you! Good to see you again!" They almost had me in tears. Perhaps they saw in my survival a hope that it might happen to them too.

"Steady a bit. Wait, wait, give me a chance. I'll tell you all the gory details when I've dumped my stuff in the tent. I'll come to the Mess. You can buy me a drink –– how about that?"

I felt a glowing from their attention, their interest in my well-being. A couple of weeks back I was a nobody, feeling like a wandering stateless, refugee, nowhere to go, disgruntled, no interest in life. Now I had a hero's welcome, a spontaneous embracing by my own kind, fellows who knew about the concentrated tension of going into a vertical bombing dive, nerves stretched like a drum skin, flak bursting everywhere, watching every dial simultaneously and the ground closing up below, hauling back violently, flinging the murderous five hundred pounders away, climbing away, clawing for safety, hoping desperately against a fatal hit on the aircraft. We were all different but we all had the same throw-of-the-dice attitude about

Our new Officers Mess, purchased from the USAF for some of our whisky ration – not much to look at, but a vast improvement on the previous one!

coming through it, never giving voice to our odds on chances. Yet they were showing me every facet of the strains we shared each time an operation was ordered and flown, showing it in the unashamed warmth of having me back. I'd survived after being shot down.

"Yes, of course," they said. "Give the poor bugger a chance! See you in the Mess – five minutes? The beer ration came in yesterday. Two bottles got your name on them." They didn't tell me then, but the two bottles of rationed beer for me were drawn in the name of Jake, who had gone missing a couple of days before. I had his empty tent space, now I was about to have his beer.

Dumping my only possessions, a kit bag half full, I walked the thirty yards from tent to the Mess hut, looking around for changes. It was all reassuringly there. I'd been missed, I was home again. It was good. It was important to me. They had embraced my return. The machine of war that picked me up, fixed me, and briefly cast me into isolation had brought me once more back into the fold.

There were changes. The pace of the conflict, its demands in human consumption were there to see when I looked closer. We had a new Squadron Commander. A dark, well built Australian, quieter of speech, almost unassuming, friendly in smile, just like his predecessor. I felt his strong and confident hand shake. He knew about me. I reached out to him instantly, he was a mature colonial type I could recognise. They said he was an ex RSM who'd transferred from the army to the RAAF at the beginning of the war. Bags of fighter squadron experience. A good type.

Five new faces had come, fresh, eager to have a go, several of them South Africans, replacements for those who'd gone down, situations unknown, two of them very close friends of mine. One had promised me his German 9mm automatic. They had held it back when packing his personal effects for next of kin, remembering it was to be mine if the worst happened. "They'd never let one of those things through anyway." It was be a memento I wanted, and a better weapon anyway than the Service issue .38 revolver we carried each time we flew.

The Mess looked good. Better than the original floppy tent, better still than out first tin hut version. The Yank Mustang Wing down the road had made some comforting contributions to the interior, via much of the month's whiskey ration. "Of course there will be little whiskey in the Mess bar for a while – but you cannot have it all ways!"

Our improvised fire exuded a comforting heat. The oil drum throbbed with internal flame as each drop of one hundred-octane petrol ignited. The Squadron's Engineering Officer was proud to show off his innovation and the Mess was pleased with the result.

Of course another spontaneous explosion like the one that demolished the previous Mess hut was never more than a splash of petrol away. He just shrugged his shoulders and said "What will be, will be!"

I had a good pull at the beer they gave me, smiled at the circle of friendly faces, settling into my tale of good fortune. The drama of baling out, being found, the journey down the mountain on the back of that donkey, in the rain and darkness, the hungrier than imagination bed bugs, the burning of my balls, the eulogy on Churchill and the King; all that had happened to me (plus a little more here and there for effect!). All was absorbed with intense interest like water into a blotting paper. Not only did they show interest, they wanted to learn from it. How did you manage that? What did you do when…? Their questioning and interest taught me several points I had not appreciated for myself, for instance, never, never would I fly again without a personal toilet kit – a toothbrush, soap, a razor, toilet paper, small things essential to a civilised survival, to maintaining morale.

"It's all different when you're out there on your own. No one to ask, no way of asking it. Those chits we have in our survival kit might be good for the first hour – save you from being shot out of hand – but useless if your captors ask "How many sugars in your tea!" They laughed their pleasure at my feeble joke.

Sleeping on a camp stretcher again after the cushion of a mattress and bed with sheets, at Sorrento, proved a challenge initially. It was cold and comfortless, the morning always hours in coming. Then there was the trudging to the open air throne boxes above the tent lines, or splashing ice cold water from my canvas bucket and walking to breakfast. I was truly home to my Spartan existence again! While I was waiting for official approval, my formal release to fly operations, I built a new bar in one corner of the Mess hut. The shelves were an exciting rainbow of coloured bottles offering a variety of hooch all negotiated on the Italian black market for our every day necessities, their everyday luxuries – soap, toilet paper, cigarettes, things like that. We had it in plenty, they had a demand in plenty for it. I adopted the role of bar officer, concocting mixtures of the bright and lively liquids we had amassed for the bar, giving them names to flight the imagination, hoping I wouldn't poison any of my mates. Some drank and enjoyed some shrugged in rejection "Yuck! What in hells is this?" The balmy Italian summer began to close in on our exposed site, vulnerable to weather change, especially rain, transforming the dry wind-blowing dust into sticky, gooey mud. Mud between the tents, mud from where we slept to the lavatory area, to the restricted inadequacies of the three Messes, Officers, NCOs and Airmen. We did what was possible to squeeze out some sort of comfort where there was precious little to enjoy: the twice-weekly truck run for hot water showers; the regular delivery of mail when it came; the distribution of personal rations.

The flight line, a rough truck ride from our domestic site/had little more to offer than aeroplanes, open air servicing, a shelter hut or two and the pierced steel planking of taxing strip and a single runway. The austerity of our set-up and those with whom we shared was a poor comparison to the USAF Mustang Wings down the road both in provision and comfort. We had but one valuable and saleable commodity they lacked – a whiskey ration; trading it hard but with great allied friendship. Our different roles, theirs to escort bombing raids deep into enemy territory with opportunities for strafing on the return, had a common denominator in the number of losses, a factor we both understood, and a bond of friendship formed between the two fighting forces.

Our American base visits offered live entertainment opportunities and we gladly accepted any invitation offered. On one occasion they surprised and delighted our sex-starved existence when some girls came on to provocatively dance and sing and the calls went up "Take it off! Take it off!" Brash, good humoured and successful. They did indeed 'take it off – posing for cameras and for those who could only enjoy frustration at seeing live, naked female bodies.

Late autumn faded into winter, with the first cold warnings, when operations across the Adriatic would be more difficult. The focus now was on 'opportunity targets' and aggressive armed recce sweeps when and where a clearance in the weather could be found. Occasionally the planes returned without making enemy contact. Other times we snapped up chance sightings, searching out the withdrawing German forces, convoys mainly, MT in long lines creeping carefully over the harsh mountain roads sheltering under cloud.

In November, eight planes found and bombed a large military convoy of trucks near Tirana reporting their five hundred pounders exploding in the target area. The pilots were unusually hesitant, unsure about damage or destruction because no 'flamers' were sighted. A few days later 'intelligence' passed a report that the same target attack had been shared with the Partisan forces almost completely wiping out a big German concentration, completely destroying all MT, killing up to one thousand German soldiers, the figures confirmed by captured enemy prisoners. The whole extensive convoy had been abandoned.

A terrible and continuous reckoning took place throughout the days of every week. It was an impersonal kind of human slaughter we executed, without having to witness the results of our work of devastation.

Squadron losses were the price paid for our higher rate of activity, with pilots baling out when the accurate German flak found our aircrafts' vulnerable weaknesses.

One of our pilots, while flying an armed weather reconnaissance, was forced to go down into the frightening snows of winter.

Struggling against the temperature and the weather in the mountains, confident he was in Partisan-held territory; he came across a small group of huts. An elderly peasant came forward to challenge this unexpected intruder. Worried, he shouted at the peasant offering his bloody safety chit. "Ja sam Britanski. Ja sam Britanski," he yelled, hearing his voice echo in the valley. "Partisan? Partisan?" he queried, wondering what would happen next, was this to be his end? The peasant held his peace and unexpectedly turned and walked into one of the huts. Our chap continued approaching cautiously, praying all was OK, apprehensive about the next move, deciding not to draw his gun. Suddenly a different peasant came out of the hut, looked hard at him for a full minute, Dammit!" he called to our pilot, "what do you want in this place?" They fed him walnuts and coarse wine, sending off a rescue message to the Partisan Headquarters.

He returned to fly again with us happy with his experience, his chance tale of good fortune almost unbelievable. Over the following weeks many were not so lucky. We marked their disappearance with a kind of unnatural tolerance, suppressing any emotion, its frequency making that impossible. Missing them for a while, but wondering who'd be next.

We were briefed for a bombing sortie at Laska followed by a strafing sweep along the railway line towards Zagreb. The leader said at briefing, "We'll dive on the bridge from five thousand out of the sun. Don't forget to select switches ON before you go down and remember to trim her out as your speed winds up. No good throwing the bombs from a skid dive. We'll pull out about one thousand reading and remember when you're strafing you are a harder target to hit if going across a flak gunners tracking. The trains are best attacked at right angles but break away in line with them if you can, it adds a huge deflection problem when you're flat out.

It worked well and the bombs erupted in bursts of destruction near the bridge without direct hits. On we swept looking for trouble and finding a locomotive at steam, a long line of trucks in tow. Lining it up for my run I saw the whole massive shape of it explode in a fountain of steam. The two ahead of me had struck well. I fired all the way in, breaking to port along the line – maximum deflection to the flak gunners, he'd said. Screwed taut, I climbed looking for the others.

The number two was low below. I swept down to join him hearing his call, "I've been hit – have a look. Seems to be working OK." A kind of prayer in his voice.

Then the leader's voice came in, "Well done chaps, good show. We got that one good and proper," as if he hadn't heard his number two's cry of distress.

It was the last we ever heard of him. He disappeared. Joining up with his number two I saw a fuselage hole behind his cockpit, superficial, no white glycol stream. I led him to the island of Vis off the Yugoslavia coastline, a safe forward Partisan-held strip, full of aircraft skeletons down each side of the runway, wrecked American bombers strewn all over the place. They, like us, had come in after being damaged. Many never got out again, metal casualties of the war. We landed as a precaution to check his plane before crossing the stretch of sea. All was OK.

The three of us got back, landed, passed our results to Spy. He knew nothing about the leader's disappearance. No news of Mayday calls, anything like that. A baffling mystery.

We drove up to the campsite, dumped our gear, had a quick meal and settled into a drink at the bar. This loss worried at us. He was one of our most experienced – and that last call of his? Hardened against our losses this one was really puzzling. We talked it over and over getting nowhere, worrying at it like a dog with a bone. We'd seen flak but not from that train attack. I'd been closer to the exploding loco after the first pair; I overflew it; it couldn't have been that, surely?

We began to talk about the Mustang's vulnerability at low level. Was there something we should be doing in our tactics; some new approach going into targets, think more about surprise in the attack? The tenseness of our lives, the mounting losses were getting more serious. The end of the war was almost in sight with the allies crashing across Europe, sweeping all before them. No one wanted to die now. Bloody hell no!

Our talk and our drinks were going down together. The Boss man came in to join us sensing some kind of concern in our conversation, "What's this? You chaps sound worried. It's happening all the time but we're giving them a very rough ride. You're on the winning side remember!"

He changed the conversation as if to switch it into a less fateful line. "I've just come back from Wing HQ. There's a special one on tomorrow, timed for twelve take off." He turned to me, "I want you to lead this one, Mac." it was a quick and sudden shock and I feared the new responsibility, but I liked it. The Squadron's chop rate had advanced me to leading. My score of locomotives, MT destroyed and damaged, had grown steadily, my time evading capture behind German lines in Greece to my credit. Now he wanted me to take a section of four and blast at a castle north of Zagreb, said to be a Gestapo HQ. They wanted four with two five hundred pounders each, instantly fused, a low show to avoid reported heavy flak. "The Gestapo are never going to be unnecessarily exposed to the likes of us. The place is said to be bristling with it, mostly light stuff. Spy will have the gen for you in the morning, say 10.00 down on the strip."

He said goodnight and left me to my thoughts for tomorrow. That ended the drinking session.

249 Sqn Mustang with shark's teeth markings.

CHAPTER 10

Red Leader

Going off in the pitch dark to my tent my thoughts roamed – make sure my personal survival kit was still complete – that train today, what a sight, erupting when hit all over the place with well aimed point-5s, spewing up its steam and smoke, the tracers bouncing and jumping all over – a spectacular sight – I'd flown through the debris, not a graze – I wonder if J caught one of our own bullets – could be – I couldn't remember if it was a passenger or freight job – everything happening faster than thought.

My stretcher was cold. The one next to it in the tight confines of the tent was Js. He wouldn't be there again, poor bugger! He might be down somewhere and come out of it? After all I had. 'But there must be some kind of Jinx in this tent', I thought. I'd secured my restricted space through a chance disappearance when I first arrived. Then my own space had been filled only to become vacant again in time for reoccupation after I came back from Sorrento. Ah well! That's how the cookie crumbles! I had a piss behind our tent, grabbed his blankets for extra insulation beneath me, wrapped another around, with another on top with my greatcoat, climbed in and slept.

The peace of my sleeping night, quick in coming, was quick in going. Hanging by my parachute shroud lines, dangling just above a circle of black coated Gestapo, each carrying a machine pistol, waiting within the inner castle keep for me to descend, I worried about my survival kit. There was no bar of soap in it. Despite the menace of their guns I refused to touch down until I was allowed to return for the soap. When I tried explaining they couldn't understand my English. I was trying to tell them I was a British officer and could not surrender without the soap. They waived the guns as I hung there in peril and motionless indecision.

I woke sweating out the problem, unsure where I was. Usually the cold coming from underneath the thin canvas of the stretcher bed woke me. Now I felt the dampness of sweat. I lay there thinking, projecting fantasies into the pitch black and completely silent night. It was a kind of premonition about going down again. The dream, vivid in detail, had been real enough to disturb me. Well! If that did happen, that's how it would be! I rolled over, my nose almost touching the damp canvas and tried saying some prayers. They did not come easily. The vague hovering fear kept imposing itself on my thoughts. I'd always thrust anything like that aside during the daylight, as God only knew there had been many times when I was scared fartless, but isolated in the damp loneliness of night it was something else. Of course I could be hit again, the flak was heavier now with the concentrations of troops in convoy, their forewarning systems stacked up against us. All that bloody fatalistic talk and that cheap Italian booze! The stress of the days flying was taking its toll. I knew it! I shook my head against the pillow. Forget it! The Partisans were controlling wider areas, there was always a good chance of finding them. I drifted back to praying, saying the words I knew over and over, like the rosary.

The next thing I knew it was less dark inside my sleeping space, daylight outside; comforting audible noises in the campsite.

It was time to go. I rushed up to the bogs for a sit, cracked the thin layer of Ice on my canvas water bucket, splashed the camp basin bag full, sloshing my face in ice cold water. Down to the Mess hut for a quick breakfast, joining the other three authorised for our sortie, already tucking into greasy egg and bacon with tasteless bean sausages.

We spoke little, more thoughtful about the day ahead than small talk would cover. The truck took us down to the flight line and our flying kit.

Spy had set up the maps and some stuff on the weather in the target area, flak anticipations, Partisan control areas, things like that. We looked very closely at the route, slightly west of north, the coastline crossing in points, the distance overland and the target area. It was going to be tough to find a mere castle on a pinnacle. Then there was the attack; four of us bombing with instantaneous fusing; a straight down dive with an awareness of one another's' positions in the stream. I was convinced my number four would meet enough flak to fill the sky like Guy Fawkes' birthday. The hornets' nest would be in a high old state of alertness. We got it all well absorbed, entered our planes, started up as briefed and away we went, climbing for cruising height, setting course for what may come.

My Mustang hummed a smooth mechanical rhythm, a reassuring set of instruments, good, the three others in wide battle formation, a comforting sight. Funny, I thought, all the tensed up butterflies vanished once I was in the air and on the way. We crossed in over the coastal islands bang on course, reaching beyond for our map checkpoints. The whole countryside below us was smothered in a blanket of pure white snow. That put paid to my route-map reading. I'd have to do it on time. Thin stratus cloud appeared in layers as we progressed inland, about five eights cover. Hell! I thought this was not going to be an easy one. My first lead of a section and all this! Estimating we must be over the target area I searched desperately for a recognisable pinpoint but saw nothing but patchy stratus and a blanket of unblemished snow through the breaks, pretty perhaps but bugger all help. We began to circle, still looking. They'd have all the time in the world to plot us. I thought I caught the 'ping' of radar. My number two called, voice pitched in excitement, "There it is, about nine o'clock, just below the cloud, on top of the hill!"

"Roger Bernie Red Two, well done."

Now what! We could not go down vertically on it, with the cloud blinding out the last few hundred feet. What to do, avoiding the instantaneous fusing?

"OK, Ernie Red, we'll make our attack from the north in loose echelon starboard. Keep it fairly close. I'll call, 'READY TO RELEASE, then the word BOMB. We'll do it together, a spread, estimating the angle to hit."

It sounded a bit wild but no other way to have a go.

"Select switches on and close in."

Round I went, careful to avoid the layered stratus, lining the place up, losing height and skimming through light cloud.

"Altering slightly to port. OK I've got it! Lined up."

Black puffs burst around us, tracer patterns curving above the pinnacle. Our welcoming reception. A thin protective layer of stratus covered the top. I went below it. It was going to be a bit hairy, and in my gut I had that familiar feeling of pitched tightness.

"Steady now, close in a little. READY TO RELEASE," guessing at the angle the five hundred pounders would travel, "BOMB!"

Instantly I felt them go from my wings. The plane bucked slightly. Flak all around. I stayed down going straight on away from the target. There wasn't a sound from any of them. They were still there. "Check in Ernie Red." "Red Two, bombs gone." "Red Three, bombs gone." "Red Four, bombs gone." "Well done, Ernie Red. I don't know where they went. Must have made a hell of a noise. Setting course for base. Call if you see anything worth a go below."

A huge sigh of relief, I sat relaxed after all that stress and tension.

Crossing over we had not seen any signs of life below. Once out over the coast going almost due south we moved into a relaxing battle spread. I knew it may not have been the most successful op we'd flown. Perhaps having a go under the adverse conditions was more of a morale booster for the partisan cause than a successful destruction of the enemy.

Wing Headquarters stood us down for a two day Christmas break. The war had human considerations after all. Like the first world war when Allies and Germans were said to have met in no mans land, greeting one another in Christian friendship for a short spell before being ordered back to their trenches, to obey the edicts from above, to slaughter one another into extinction.

It was a fine time. All meals for the day were printed in a specially decorated menu card. A souvenir to mark the festivity. It depicted a snorting and bucking mustang, with a riding pilot on top, the food listed inside for the three meals of the day to a standard we had not seen forever. At midday the officers served the airmen their lunch with the traditional fare they expected. An extra beer ration all around. The cooks excelled and we waited upon our airmen's every

249 Squadron Christmas Day Menu, 1944.

wish. Shrugging off their opportune remarks, smiling for this special, once a year event.

Every pilot on the Squadron knew without doubt they owed their lives to those below us in rank and privileges. Their lives were a harder, more demanding, existence, yet they were no less human, no more immune to pain and sadness, stress and discomfort. They were important people and while we flew in this war they were indispensable members of our Squadron. I felt nothing but pleasure when here and there during our serving of their Christmas lunch I received a "Good on yer FIJI!" It was recognition and I was a proud recipient of it.

One of my jobs as an officer was to censor their letters, written to family at home, wives, sweethearts, mums, sisters. It was an insight to their character. Seldom did I find any cause to take up an erasing pen to strike out moans about their lives.

With the real onset of winter through the month of January the Squadron's commitments stepped up. From the third to the twenty-fifth we flew fifty three sorties against a wide range of targets. Dive bombing the communication links so vital to the German forces withdrawing from the Balkans; going at the bridges, the railway depots and sidings, locomotives, the most spectacular targets, railway rolling stock, steaming and flying at speed. MT convoys, a frequent massed target, moving or stationery, on the road, camouflaged, entering the long tunnels to hide away from us. It was all there inviting our destruction. We tried blocking the tunnels with their casualties never sure whether it worked.

Every attack drew heavy and light flak, not knowing when the stray 20mm cannon shell would find its mark. They were good at it. Hearing us coming; especially those foolhardy enough to repeat a strafing run. Often intense barrages filled every space of the sky, with menacing black puffs, a lethal wall of deadly exploding shells. The great curved scoop of the Mustangs under fuselage radiator almost invited a hit. We flew weather recces early, checking out potential target areas for an attack later in the day; on other occasions looking for early morning, opportunity targets, locomotives and moving MT chancing their arm into a new day hoping to get wherever it was before our marauding Mustangs blasted at them.

February started wild and intense until the fateful twenty sixth of the month when I flew my last operational sortie of World War II. We had flown fifty-two sorties in challenging weather conditions, mostly layered stratus from ten and fifteen thousand downwards, adding a new hazard to our already hazardous existence. Occasionally bad weather meant aborting a mission, dumping the live five hundred pound bombs into the sea on the way home – in war such expense was no object, and preferable to landing with live bombs instantaneously fused.

During a quiet period, grounded by weather for a few days, I went off to bed early, fed up, bored by the days of inactivity. The stimulus of flying sorties denied us. We'd exhausted the limited diversions, played poker for vast sums of lira, switched to cribbage and had a few. It was always a long day. Outside the Mess hut it was bitterly cold, a cutting wind. I fastened down the tent entrance flaps, almost excluding the biting draught, wrapped every available item of spare clothing around me, insulating the canvas bed as best I could and climbing in, fell asleep.

At some time in the night I woke to an eerie sense of silence which disturbed me. Outside the tent it was always soundless during the night hours but tonight something else was there, I could sense it. But what? Stirring, not warm enough to fall back to sleep I got up and went outside for a piss. The whole camp area around me reflected a visible glow. Every part of the site had been covered by a heavy fall of snow. The canopy over my tent sagged dangerously with the added weight. It was freezing cold outside. I tried shaking it off, tightening the guy ropes. It was immovable, frozen. There was nothing to be done. The inside of the tent was warmer with the insulation from the snow and the closed in heat of my body. I got back into bed and, eventually, slept again.

The morning brought a transformed life from the change all around us. Yelling and throwing snowballs, the novelty was something of a natural tonic. Later in the day we built a full sized snow woman, beautiful uptilted breasts, little stone nipples, the lot. She was cold but shapely!

The change in weather was a welcome diversion from our focussed lives. We delighted in volley ball in the snow, snowball fights, until it ran its course, nothing to do, nowhere to go, we could but endure and live it out.

A visit to the USAF Mustang Fighter Wing found them in the same mould and happy to see our faces. They had more going in the way of films and the swapping of different experiences. The days drifted by.

"Yeh! me too. I'll have one of those terrible coloured mixtures you grace with the name of 'happy oblivion'". He was answering my invitation from behind the bar to a fresh round of drinks. We had exhausted the beer ration, done a good service to what was left of the whisky and gin now we were forced to fall back on our stock of Italian 'firewater'. At least it had the advantage of different colours for different flavours, but that was about all! The B Flight Commander stood, stretched his arms wide, yawned and distributed my handiwork around the table. It was a relaxed time.

After our evening meal we had been briefed for the dawn recce I had been authorised to lead. Take off was to be at 0800. Get up time,

Three members of the 249 Squadron Ground Crew, 1944.

sparrow fart, cold and comfortless. No breakfast, no tea available. Two hours flight time, back in time for an early lunch.

We settled down to the favourite night-time games. Sitting around the table shuffling the cards making ready to outwit one another at seven-card stud; fours, whores and one-eyed Jacks wild. No one ever explained why we had to make it so difficult. The bets were always scaled up with the low value of the lira to the pound, the losses always small. It felt good to bet in thousands. We went at it seriously, watching for cheating, like hawks. Without suggestion or discussion it came to its usual end. I had fixed a round of drinks on my winnings in thousands of lira. The cards were put away for another day. We sat sipping the drinks, frowning as each sip passed over the palate, exaggerating the unwelcome flavours.

Setting off for my last ever Mustang op of World War II.

"Dammit man! What bloody awful stuff! Can't you mix some other kind of combination?" someone jibed, knowing full well that we had tried often but without success.

The hut had a cosy warmth about it generated by the intermittent flash of exploding flame within the forty-gallon oil drum. Each drip of volatile petrol giving off its instant contribution of heat before vanishing.

"One of these days..." I said, pointing at the drum against the side of the hut, leaving my sentence unfinished. No need to tell them what I was saying, referring to the explosion last time something had gone wrong inside it. Nobody added anything, they welcomed the warmth it gave us.

I felt an uncertainty about leaving the cosiness all around me to venture outside, to splash through the slush, take off the least possible amount of clothing and get down on to that chill stretcher bed in my tent, to leave the electrically lit Mess for the damp darkness of my bed space. They were a warm-hearted bunch, companions more than acquaintances. We knew so much about one another, every little idiosyncrasy. Occasionally we had quarrel; due to strain or a sheer cussedness of character that got out of control. It blew up and disappeared quickly, fearing the censure of the majority. Above all we had a clear sense of our lives together, our vulnerability, our fears, our sense of duty towards one another.

"I can't sit around here like you lazy buggers. We operational pilots have got work to do in the morning." I said with mock haughtiness. Holding my nose, I downed my concoction in one full swig. An early start demanded an early night.

"Night you chaps." I heaved myself to my feet. Pocketing the rest of my nights winnings, I walked to the door and pushed it open, "Its bloody cold out there," I said, and went into the blackness.

It was the last time I would see them in World War II...

CHAPTER 11

Down to Earth Again

Trudging my way to the tent, trying to avoid the unseen slush in its deeper places I felt strangely odd. When you haven't got a home, a nearly bare tin hut with a warming fire is paradise; when you haven't got any food a slice of bread is a treat. I had so much affection for them, so much loyalty to the Squadron. Yet there was no comfort, no sheltering haven for uncertain emotions when they surfaced. I had lessons to come that would erase any kind of reasoning logic that I'd ever known before in my short life as a Royal Air Force fighter pilot. I woke feeling clammy. The half-light of the early morning, had a gloomy touch to it. A light dusting of overnight snow had rubbed out the tracks and footprints of the previous day. I couldn't put my finger on it, but there was something indefinably different about this day, a strange elusive feel about it.

I quickly went through the standard ritual, a call up the slope to the bogs, breaking the ice from the top of the bucket, a splash that sent shivers down my back, a swift comb of my hair in the minute mirror hanging from the centre tent pole. I was ready to go. Feeling my chin for bristles? No it wasn't one of my twice-weekly shaving days yet. The other chap, J, my number two, was waiting.

"Hi, there," I called, clambering over the tail board of the fifteen hundred weight truck, "sleep well?"

"Yeah, fine," and he said no more. It wasn't a chatty kind of time.

We rattled down the hill to the airstrip, deserted except for the couple of groundcrew to see us off. I felt subdued, shivering a bit, partly apprehension, the same old feeling until I got airborne, partly the damp coldness of the day.

Looking skywards was not encouraging, A low cloud cover, pale purple in the new sunrise. I knew an usual tension, a fiery kind of feeling in my gut. We ran over flight details, target area information, a final briefing before going to our respective plane dispersals.

Once in, getting the thumbs up from my aircraft mech, I started her up throbbing into power giving life. It all looked good. A quick half throttle run, I waved him away, moved her forward, back tracking along the strip for take off. J joined me, swinging in behind. My turn first.

Soon I wound on the full power my concentration settled to the task, the PSP sections rattling beneath me, gaining speed, lifting off, turning port, climbing on course for cruising height, going higher to avoid the lower layers of stratus. He called in a clear R/T check.

"Reading you five by five Red Two," a cryptic exchange, no further need for R/T talk.

Watching the altimeter register increases in height I looked over my warm cockpit. D-Delta was a perfection of throbbing power, my specially designed Fiji emblem newly painted below the cockpit. I'd never have the chance to add swastikas below, there as was no Luftwaffe in the Balkan skies to shoot down. It looked good anyway. I'd given the airmen a couple of packets of fags for his handiwork.

I kept up a constant monitoring of the instruments, glancing at J out there, keeping measured battle formation station, listening to the loud purring of engine vibration, senses alert for any changes in performance, everything spot on. It was reassuring, good to feel pride in my status, leading operational sections. I liked to lead, to make the decisions, face up the challenges as they came. This was going to be a good one, a bit of a doddle if the weather allowed.

Spy's information had been vague. "They want you to look for shipping, or shipping movement. Could be one ship or even several small ones. The word is something's going on around the islands up near Fiume harbour. If you find anything they'll probably send in the medium bomber boys to take it out. Watch it though. Fiume has a known concentration of Germans, could be a lot of flak. If there are ships its likely they will add to that."

On we went, seeing the lower layers of stratus thin and disappear in the warming sun, the sea below us flat and cold as we passed from the gloom of first morning light into a lightening overcast. Levelling off at fourteen thousand feet, we swept in above the target area. I flicked a questing eye across the bay below. I couldn't but admire its picture postcard setting; all seemed calm and innocent-looking. We were too high to make out any small detail but the first glint from the rising sun, just touching it, showed up Fiume's main features. Great purple mountains, a backdrop to the harbour town, tumbled in massive lumps right down to the glassy surface of the Adriatic Sea.

Clustered buildings spread upwards, a pattern of roads interwoven amongst them, the line of coast curving around the small harbour inlet, our primary focus of interest. The Germans were first class when it came to camouflage. If we wanted a real look, it would have to be from lower down. Lower down meant flak height. The scene was so peaceful. I was tempted to go down to find out what Spy's chaps wanted to know, but that undisturbed peace could erupt into hellfire. From where we slowly swept along nothing was likely to bother us. Heavy flak was not known in these parts. Down there it could be something else. I'd flown through curtains of the stuff, had it all around me, and come out, clean as a whistle.

The only way to hit this would be as we'd been briefed: power dive from the east, coming out of the sun, flat out, everything wide open for speed, right down to zero feet above the sea, crossing their flak lines of fire, maximum deflection for the gunners. If Spy's vague lines of information were anywhere near the mark we'd have a great chance, not just to see boats in the harbour but count the buggers. It looked like a small cluster around the jetty, possibly E Boats, too small to be sure from fourteen thousand. Yes! I was convinced that had to be the way. One flashing high speed pass, sweeping beyond flak range before they could get a good shot at us.

Knowing they would be in the highest state of alert, having heard and possibly seen us up above, I moved well away up sun, J keeping station wondering what I might do about this one. He would be more vulnerable following up my attack, trailing behind me.

I banked around, and had a good view of the central harbour. My heartbeat accelerated by three or four thousand revs, and there was that taut stretched feeling in my stomach again. Switching gunsight ON and guns to ALL FIRE, I called "Red Two – We'll go down and take a look see. One high-speed diving pass. Look for ships in the harbour, follow me in wide trail."

It was like we'd agreed; straightforward recce drill, but the flutters were there in my gut.

"Going down – NOW!" I pressed the transmit button and rolled D-Delta up and over into a full power dive. The plane responded as if knowing that I wanted to survive this one, trimming her out against the building forces of acceleration I rocketed for the sea, judging to flatten out before reaching the harbour. Straightening my line of flight slightly to starboard, every fibre of me in focus, fixed on the deceptively quiet picture coming at me through the windscreen. I aligned the sight for the dead centre of the harbour. We roared powerfully down through thousands of feet in split seconds, conscious every moment that potential danger lay in wait. They hated me, they were scared and they were trained and dedicated to kill me. Real German strength was in that place. I could feel it remotely, at the back of my concentrating mind. I had fear too, but I was trained and dedicated to kill them – if needs be.

At fifteen hundred feet, knowing J would be behind me and lower, flattening out my descent, I eased down slowly, going lower Just above the glittering reflection of sea. I spotted the ships in an instant. Four of them snuggled against the jetty, well camouflaged, nestling in repose, apparently lifeless. They were E Boats, full of light flak and highly trained sailors of the Reich. Just like Spy had said. There was shipping here all right, very menacing shipping. I could confirm his information. Our sortie was almost over; but not yet!

I squeezed the trigger grip, a long deadly burst from my six point fives, stabbing and leaping in spurts of water, across, around, over the Jetty and the E Boats, tearing at their peaceful mooring. In my intensity I kept firing until I'd almost swept over the top of them. Too fast for a real sight of the damage, knowing J would be adding his deadly measure to mine. "Check, Red Two – four of them?" snapping the transmission out in my fever pitched excitement. My heart beating fit to burst. "Going port, climbing for return to base.

OUT" He would be concentrating, no need for more words; I didn't want to distract him. I pushed the stick over, banking swiftly, leaving the harbour and its danger behind. I pulled back, my nose pointing out to the open sea, almost beginning to relax, knowing we were fast leaving flak range behind, urging D-Delta on, away from it. The thought crossed my mind, yes! The bombing chaps could come in now with a certainty of knocking out that lot. Make a good cluster-bombing target. Dangerous little swine to be sweeping up and around the island chain. Might save them a long and perilous trip down the Adriatic and home through the Med to Germany. Some hope to make that! Should be grateful for a quick end, the life pounded out of them!

"FLAK – Flak – Flak – Flak, coming up six o'clock, thick, all around you," J's voice shocked me, cutting into my wandering thoughts, instantly refocusing my stretched mind to the situation in hand. The sky all around full of bursting black puffs, seeming to announce a momentary challenge in the sky on every side, floating harmlessly away. Like a deadly scattering of metal confetti. Must be the E Boats or something? Pretty heavy stuff. Probably forty mill quick-firing. J's call had the sound of surprise, affronted that they should be retaliating with evil purpose.

I saw colours, black, red and yellow balls, some floating beyond, terminating even as I flew through them. ' Dear God! I thought not now, five more minutes, I'd be out of range, the lethal hail left behind me, impotent'.

I weaved the plane violently in flight, evading desperately, shaking free of the threat, strung to full pitch. If any exploding shell had my name on it I'd not be in that patch of sky when it reached me – I hoped! Determined with all my frightened being to escape I sensed a thump, imposed across my steel tight nerves. Nothing more than a vague registering, yet distinctive. A positive sensation unusual in D-Delta. Like the plane had received a kick up the arse. It had to be flak in my rear end. I had made a fatal mistake in breaking into a line of concentrating fire. Should have stayed on a track across it until well clear. Disobey a cardinal rule and you might have a cardinal consequence.

How bad was it? What had it done to me? There was no way of telling. Instinctively I kept her going, climbing up and away from the bursting puffs, clawing with all my might for as much height as I could get, weaving all the time, my life depending on it, waiting, scared to see any reaction, heart going at a thousand beats, the fear stabbing into my tightening guts.

"Red Two, I've been hit. Going straight on, climbing. Out of range now, in the clear. Can you see anything?" I tumbled the words at him, willing him to come in, look me over, and say, 'nothing there'. Climbing in deadly earnest, reaching still higher above the dark, surface calm down below, I watched over the instruments, daring an indication of a problem. Couldn't be an engine failure. I'd had my share of that. Thank God! so far, so good. May be only a flesh wound in the silver fuselage. Maybe I'd be OK to get back across that long stretch of Adriatic Sea. Please God, make it so, a silent fervent prayer. I waited.

J closed in sweeping from out of starboard, reassuring, going out of sight behind me, swooping up the other side, holding me in suspense, he took a good look. His message crackled into my R/T, apologetic, cold, a fatal inevitability to it. Dear God, the words echoing in my ears "You're trailing white smoke Red One – a lot of it. Looks like glycol. A hit in your radiator, big black hole." My whole being shuddered in revulsion. There it was, all over again. The worst message I could have known. That bloody great big radiator, D-Delta's Achilles heel. I was for it and no mistake. I knew and I was very frightened that I was going out into that menacing sea below, nothing was more certain, nothing could save me.

The full frightening pattern of the last time I had baled out filled my mind. How was I going to do it now? This day had a terrible feel to it, right from when I got up.

Now what had I got left? the engine still throbbing away, giving me climbing speed. "Keep going you bastard!"

Twelve thousand, thirteen thousand, fourteen thousand. "Come on, come on!" I tried to push the inevitable aside, "Keep going, keep going! Don't overheat!" I muttered, in forlorn hope. I throttled back a touch, compromising between engine temperature and climbing speed. My mind was wandering wildly, flashing across the instruments, checking speed, height, revs, engine temp. God! What a mess! With every fibre I was hoping that by some miracle I might be saved from my inevitable plunge out of the merciless sky into the dark sea below.

The engine temperature gauge began to spell out its initial anguish, the indicator needle slowly creeping around the dial; it passed NORMAL, climbing through the red MAXIMUM segment as I watched, transfixed. Momentarily, it hesitated before moving into the DANGER quadrant, bouncing off the stop pin, sweeping back to zero in one mortal movement of surrender, its awful meaning plain to see. The end was with me once again.

With that, my mind seemed to calm and concentrate. Perhaps it was going to be easier because I'd done it all before, perhaps that made me all the more fearful, knowing what I would have to do in order to get out of the plane in one piece and to get back to base again. Even now, in this moment of extreme danger I knew no other wish than to return to my squadron. But first I must live, leave the plane safely, survive the temperature of the winter Adriatic waiting cold and deep below me. My big Merlin engine up front was still working, but beginning to miss, revs dropping off, stuttering.

"Red Two – I have to go out – baling out – the engines going." A pitiful message. He knew it anyway, flying a little more than a wingspan away. I knew the calibre of that man. If he could have put me on his back and carried me home, whatever the consequences, he would most assuredly have done so.

The four big life giving propeller blades, up front on D-Delta, gradually slowed, shuddering to a fatal full stop. I had the sensation of watching a recurring nightmare, hesitating, almost hypnotised by fear. A moment ago the powerful engine thrust transmitted through that whirling fan had given me fast flight and strength to fight in the sky, now it was no more than a deadly aerodynamic baffle, impeding what remained of vital flying speed. At fifteen thousand D-Delta juddered with the onset of a stall. I pushed the stick forward, picking up a few extra knots, losing a few hundred precious feet of height, spinning now would be fatal. "Mayday – Mayday – Mayday!" plaintively spelling out my end, confident the unseen radio listeners would hear it and have all the information they needed to alert the Air Sea Rescue boys and get them flying out to pluck me from the sea. Forcing my fear down, trying to calm myself, to think out what I must do. I called again.

"Red Two – going out now – Cheers mate, stick around, as long as you can – need a guardian angel!"

He came back loud and clear, "Good Red..."

I heard no more, the rest of his message vanishing as I rolled her over, pushed the stick forward, violently and fell into the emptiness of space. Once again I experienced that sudden, enveloping sensation of nothingness, weightlessness, no downward movement, no sound but the gentle swishing of the shroud lines over my head, the umbrella chute slapping gently. It was all so familiar and I knew I did not want to go through it again. This was deadly earnest, the open sea stretched out endlessly below me, dark, deep and mercilessly cold.

The downward-plunging silver shape of D-Delta caught my eye as it spiralled below me. I watched as my mortally wounded bird dived to its fate, slowly twisting through its last seconds before it slamming into the mirror surface of the sea, the extinguishing hiss reaching all the way up to me as it disappeared into a watery oblivion. It was a sad, sad ending, leaving a widening circle of white foam ripples fanning outwards from an oily centre. I had a grandstand view of a sight I had no wish to see.

As I rapidly descended, though still without any perceptible downward movement, towards the sea surface miles from any shore, I tried to take stock, to think what I must do to survive. I was a strong swimmer but this was a stretch of wide-open sea. How was I going to get out of it? Reaching up, I crossed over hands, pulling with all the strength I had, trying to turn the canopy, searching for land behind me. I was half successful; it had all seemed so easy with an instructor in the gymnasium at operational training school, but now he wasn't here to correct my faults. Through a blue haze I saw the coastline of an island, great barren hills folding into the sea, lifeless and distant. I tried to remember the instructor again, and the lessons he had tried to drum into our disinterested minds; the wet dinghy drills that we treated as half a joke, half a frolic – who was going to need them anyway? The vital points came rushing to my mind in a race against my rapid descent.

"Inflate your Mae West jacket – rotate your parachute harness box ready to bash it for quick release just above the water – not too high or you may fall out of the chute, not too low or the canopy might cover you and make your struggle for survival all the more difficult – knees tightly together, slightly bent, feet braced together, hitting the water, even with the chute restraining your plunge in, will be a shock – brace your whole body – with your left hand hold your nose against the rush of water strike the quick release box a hard blow with your right. If it all goes well you'll enter the water, bob up like a cork, the canopy collapsing away and not helping to drown you."

His words darted through my mind like flashes of lightning as I tried to assemble all the points before the fearful experience overtook me. This was no game, no rehearsal; I must do it right, and in the right sequence, to live.

He always left the real point of climax to last.

"With a bit of luck you could be in your dinghy in two minutes – It might be all you've got if the sea is very cold."

The way he had spelt it out in humdrum monotone had been dull, falling mostly on deaf ears. Thank God some of it had registered.

I looked down at the sea below. There was still no indication that I was descending, no way to measure my distance from the surface, but I knew from the experience of my previous jump that it was only a matter of seconds. Rotating the quick release harness box, I waited, mindful of the danger facing me, watching anxiously as the last few hundred feet rushed by – no time for thinking, no time for worrying, the reality of the dreaded moment was here. Now!

The dark surface of the sea raced up at an alarming speed; too quick to think, too quick to time the sequences. I bashed hard at the flat metal disc of the harness quick-release box as I plunged down, down into the instant coldness of water, forgetting to hold my nose or keep my knees half bent, registering only going down into the drowning depths, the sea closing over me, the icy temperature attacking my body in shock. The canopy of my life-saving parachute had collapsed over me. Breathlessly I bobbed up again, 'like a cork surfacing' just as he had said, into a tangled mess of shroud lines and sodden silk, which threatened to keep me from survival.

I fought and thrashed against it, using every ounce of my strength to free myself, the cord lines twisting around my legs, restricting movement, my flying boots full of heavy water. Somehow I came clear. Thank God for the buoyancy of my Mae West.

Where was the dinghy pack? At the end of it's attachment somewhere under the canopy, sinking under its own weight. With another struggling effort, it came to hand. I could feel the cold creeping up my legs with my every pause for breath. I pulled at the heavy sodden mass of the dinghy, ripped open the popping studs, fumbled about the compact folds, felt for the metal shape of the pressure bottle and twisted the quick release valve. My fingers were getting numb, but I was determined with all my will to make it, praying silently for success. The dinghy swished and mushroomed into shape, smoothing out the wrinkles, as it grew, I willed it to get bigger. It was half inflated. Plunging and kicking, frog like, I struggled into its soft receptive folds, my green dye sea marker staining the water all around me as the water took on its colour. I turned my body, feeling my legs stiffening with the coldness. The dark green dyed water sloshed into the dinghy, half submerging it.

The bellows, where were the bellows? Yes, there they were, folded and fastened down at my side, right where they should be. Prising away the holding studs I squeezed the concertina shape, testing, puffing out short blasts of air. I plugged it into the dinghy inlet valve, pumping, hard as I could go. The folds around me stiffened, gradually taking shape but without rigidity, enough to float well. Next, using the canvas cup I baled frantically, emptying out the cold, dyed-green water sloshing around me. The activities to secure my position helped to hold the numbing coldness at bay. I paused, sitting a minute, breathing heavily. Next the paddles. I couldn't rest inactive waiting to be frozen in shock. Pulling first at the dinghy covering I fastened it over my legs to the waist, slipped numbed fingers over the two bat-like paddles, securing the elastic bands up over my wrists ready to go. The shore, I had to make for the shore. Floating out here, exposed to the weather was not on. I tried to gauge the daunting distance to the closest island and knew, however far, I must make it there.

CHAPTER 12

The Rescue That Never Was

Looking up, I saw my faithful number two, J, lazing around in wide orbits, throttled back to conserve his fuel, watching over me from on high, a reassuring sound and sight in an otherwise soundless world about me.

He was an extra encouragement to survival, up there, looking down, willing me to make it to safety. His just being there was a great help.

I felt coldness creeping over me. I knew that sitting still and hoping would produce no results. My instructor's words came back to me: "At all costs keep active – keep going – stimulate your circulation – get to dry land if at all possible." Everything was stained a ghastly pea green, my clothes, my hands, my head, my face, as was the whole sea area around me a great patch of green, spreading in every direction. No one could possibly miss all that…

I turned the dinghy in the direction of the island and thrust down both paddles together, sweeping eddies of water towards my numbed feet, forcing my floppy shape along with all the strength left to me. I kept at it, arms aching, with just one aim – to shorten that distance between the shoreline and myself. I fixed it in my mind; dip, swish, dip, swish; forget about fatigue, keep going, keep paddling, dip, swish, dip swish, aching arms thrusting less powerfully as time moved on.

Stopping to rest I looked skywards to see him again. Lucky bugger! He was free as a bird while I was cold and soaked, stinking green dye all over me, depressed with my situation. What could he do for me? Paddling on again, dip, swish, dip swish, shoulders dull with pain, arms almost dropping off I went at it again, turning the dinghy to see how close it was. An onshore wind was helping. I could make out clear shapes on barren hillside – not far to go. It gave me the heart to keep at it. Dip, swish, dip, swish again. How could anything be so hard? How long had I been doing it? J had gone and I hadn't even noticed it. There was another sound from somewhere up there. Searching with squint through salt-soaked eyes I spotted two Spitfires in loose echelon to starboard, circling around and giving me good overhead protection. 'You beauts!' I thought. Then on again: dip, swish, dip swish, keep at it, not long to go now, not much left to do it with either. Surely the Air Sea Rescue Catalina must show soon?

I stopped, my arms like lead, muscles without feel; no strength to go on. The dip swish had become mechanical, but now even that was beyond me. Patting the water on one side I slowly turned the dinghy to face the shoreline. How far had I come? Where was everything now? To my surprise I was very close. The wind had skimmed me along the surface. The sombre mass of land towered above me, bare and barren. Nothing to see but sparse shrub creeping up its steep sides, beckoning me on, mocking my efforts to get there, teasing me with the last short distance, a challenge to live. I had almost given up, saturated with seawater through and through, the green dye from the sea marker had seeped into everything. Most of all I was very cold, conscious of nothing more than wet and coldness.

Adjusting the two bat paddles again, sweeping the eddies of water, I thrust for dry land, pushing at it, forcing the dinghy on to cover that last few hundred yards to the shore. I had to do it. I had to do it. Dip, swish, dip, swish. Slower this time, keeping at it, resting a bit, starting up, aching limbs, arms dropping off, the distance reducing, on and on, gritting my teeth, fighting against giving up the struggle. It seemed like hours since I had floated down and crashed through the hard surface of water, but it couldn't be, the Catalina hadn't arrived yet. How I wanted that plane above to come down for me.

I sensed, more than heard, water lapping on the rocks behind me, rising, receding, beating out a message of safety, giving me encouragement to make the last few yards. Not daring to look around, knowing I was close, I paddled some more, sure I would touch at any moment, desperate to make it.

The soft nose of the dinghy bumped, rising and falling away with the swell of the waves. At last I was there, thank God, but my body refused to move. I sat there, frozen and spent, gasping lungful after lungful of air in exhaustion, without much feeling, almost overwhelmed physically, my mind working still to survive. I had to do something. I was there now, actually touching the dry land. What next? Glory be! I was safe... almost! Now I must try to gather up enough strength to make a grab at the smooth surface of the forbidding rock, and clamber out on to it.

Breathing deeply, I tried to force some sensation back into my numb legs. Suddenly, I heard faint voices in the distance, above the lapping and gurgling of sea around me. Shouts, rising and falling coming from some unseen place up the sparsely covered slope. Nothing was in sight, not a solitary moving thing. I waited, tense, too tired to think straight, wondering who it was. Then I saw people moving, two of them, men in grey uniforms, rifles slung across their backs, gabbling as they came, arms waving wildly at me, talking in words; words I could not make out or understand. They sounded like Italians. They were talking at me, to me, to one another, showing excitement, coming on, half sliding down the slope in their eagerness to reach me. I waved back half-heartedly, a tentative response, not sure what this meant, not sure I could do anything about it anyway. I was vulnerable, half-scared.

Down they came, carefully sliding onto the slippery rocks, still talking endlessly. I knew they were Italians. Only Ities, of all people, would go on and on like that without knowing if I could understand anything they said! I couldn't. I just sat there, more or less helplessly, waiting for them to pull me out, trying to indicate what they had to do. It was hopeless. Reaching for the dinghy one of them almost fell into the water, the other shouting at him like a bloody clown. Stupid oafs, I thought, with an almost reviving chuckle.

"Get me out of here. Lift me out of the dinghy. I can't move my legs. Frozen!" Sign language accompanied my desperate words. Still gabbling at one another and at me, they managed to get hold of the dinghy's flap, slowly heaving it to a flatter surface. The talking never stopped even while they tugged and hefted my sodden body clear of the green sloshing water.

It was something to be out of it, the surface of the rock warm and welcome. I encouraged them to pummel my legs, supporting me to stand up, force the circulation back, feel human again.

"Si, si!" They knew what I was on about, their actions full of outward friendship. They wanted to help, to do what they could, but the words tumbling from them were still incomprehensible. Others came down the slope shouting at my two rescuers; replies called back. Then a new voice.

"Hello, friend, you English flyer? I see you aeroplane crash into sea, you parachute down."

At last, someone who could understand me. I stood up unaided, glad to do so, feeling weak-kneed but upright and above all actually feeling something! Green water dripped from me, wetting the rocks. I sat down, pulled off my squelching flying boots and emptied out the water. The fleece lining was green. Every bloody thing about me was green!

"Yes, yes," I called at him, looking over the cluster of them, all armed but with rifles slung, no signs of aggression, plenty of welcoming smiles here, talking between them and at me. Uncertain how to go on I pointed at the first two, who were busy pulling the dinghy clear of the water, emptying it out, fascinated with it.

"These very good men. They pull me out of the water. Very cold." I wrapped my arms around my body to indicate getting warm. The two looked up from examining the dinghy, grinning widely without knowing what I'd said. He translated and they waved as if shrugging it off, saying, 'nothing to it'

Getting my senses together, I realised all was going very well. I must keep the situation on good terms. They were undoubtedly soldiers in uniform, but whose soldiers? This was German-held territory? Perhaps they were Partisans holding out on these islands?

The chattering in Italian went on but quietened for the English speaker. "It nothing, friend. We like English. We glad help you. We Italian not like Germans. I in America plenty years, my mother sick, I come see her, war start and I can no go back."

That put him into perspective. It was a familiar story I had heard before in Greece. He went on, the others staying quiet, listening, watching him speak, hands gesticulating expansively with each phrase of words, as only the Italians know how. "When you aeroplane come, take you home, we all go back inside?" A sweeping gesture embracing his fellow men, standing around me. "You take us in plane, back to Italia – yes?"

I couldn't believe what he was saying. They wanted to be my prisoners of war, asking me to fit them into the Air Sea Rescue plane – which would probably be a Catalina, maybe be something smaller? The idea was most acceptable, suited me well. I smiled, showing it had my blessing. Their friendship, and the idea of not only being rescued but having a bunch of prisoners into the bargain, helped me to feel good again, damp and green though I was. There were eight of them. A Catalina could manage that. Or could it? Not to worry, my spirits rose. Sitting on the rocks waiting I looked up, the Spitfire IXs were still there orbiting at about five thousand, going round and round overhead. They'd protect me until the Air Sea Rescue plane arrived, on the smoothness of the sea picking me off the shore – with them, of course. From up there they could see me. They knew where I was safe. No one would menace me. They carried eight, twenty mill cannons between them. My damp wetness lightened. Just sit there and wait, slowly drying out in the warming sun.

Talking to the one who knew English I asked, "What you do here? What your work?" He was only too pleased to tell.

"Germans make us soldiers, we stay here for two week, watch American bombers fly to Germany, with big glasses, we tell how many, which way they going. We have telephone for this. "

"Ah, yes," I answered, "You are an observer outpost for the Germans." He nodded, knowing what I had said. We were silent for a few minutes while he told the others what we had exchanged.

My mind raced. They had a telephone into the German reporting system on the mainland. That was not good. A threat?

"The Germans will come. They see me jump out of aeroplane?" I put it to him, calmly as I could manage. It was a serious possibility. I waited while he talked to the others about it. Were they compromising their own situation I wondered? Caught at it by the Germans would not be well received – to say the least!

He told me their families lived in Fiume across the Bay. They would return there after doing their stint on the island. 'Yes,' it occurred to me, the families were held there in hostage while these guys, forced into uniform, were at their observation post duties I wondered?

"If Germans see you aircraft crash, see you parachute out, they ring on telephone, ask if we see you? They not ring today so not see you. They not come here." He sounded confident about the situation. I hoped he was right. He told me their German masters visited the outpost only once a month, adding they had done their inspection last week. It was OK.

I calmed down. He told me again the Germans were never quiet if they wanted to know anything going on. Happened all the time when the bomber streams were going into Germany.

Tired and hungry, sitting there in shock, feeling uncomfortable, I realised my forty-five automatic had gone. Must have been whipped away when I went out. It was on a smart-arse low-slung holster. A thirty-eight would have been more securely attached to my webbing belt. Ah well! Who knew how they would have reacted to my being armed? Their own rifles, taken off now looked like pretty ancient musketry. I took off my Mae West and quietly felt for my personalised survival kit. It was all there, soap, toothbrush, razor and very sodden toilet paper, not much use now.

The conversation had died down. A few desultory exchanges between them. The idea of taking them POWs was a nice thought. Why not? It could work very well. I'd heard someone had got a 'gong' for doing that earlier on.

We sat scattered over the rocks waiting, hoping, believing something good was yet to come. It was clearly a big moment for the Italians. Did they really believe they were to be taken back to Italy? What about the families held to hostage he had told me about? Seemed a strange set up. If they were to be suddenly taken into the Catalina and transported into a completely different life there was little in their behaviour to show it. Best left alone, I thought, until the plane actually arrived.

Their quiet murmuring around me suddenly stopped, everyone listening intently in silence to the first distant droning of an aeroplane engine, faint, vibrant in the afternoon air, it grew to a steady beat. A blessed noise throbbing out of the sky from the far-stretched ocean. We all tensed to it, scanning with keen eyes every inch of the horizon, eager to see it materialise into shape and form.

One of them stood up, gesticulating, shouting his excitement, pointing an outstretched arm, signalling where it was. He was right, I saw it too, a bee sized speck, low down above the water, coming towards us at sea level, the drumming of engines increasing with every second. My heart leapt with the joy of it. We all started jumping up and down, looking at one another, waving, pointing it out. I collected myself sufficiently to remember the signal, rushing for my survival pack in the dinghy, ripping out one of the red Very light cartridges. Fingers trembling with expectation I tore off the seal, thrusting it above my head, shooting the flare into a curving arc, showing him where I was standing, waiting. The plane banked, changing course to our direction, a beautiful Catalina flying boat. All for me – and my prisoners.

They were overhead as the Very light spent itself, plunging into the sea. The fighter escort circled above. All was well. The Catalina passed close above us turning out to sea.

Ah yes! I thought, circling to make his approach, alighting towards us, taxiing in to take us all aboard. I was on my way home to safety, secure at the sight of my own friends of the Royal Air Force. Thank God for my good fortune again. Almost unbelievable luck, twice shot down, twice rescued from the clutches of the Germans.

But he did not come down. From his position out to sea he started flashing an Aldis signal lamp. I missed the first time round, catching the repeat of his message. 'COME OUT TWO HUNDRED YARDS.'

He was asking me to go out two hundred yards from the shoreline to be picked up. I spelled out his sequence of short and long flashes, my amazement growing with each word I read. Surely, he wasn't asking me to do that! He must know I couldn't. I was here, on dry land, waiting and ready. All they had to do was come down onto the smoothness of the calm sea, taxi gently into our sheltered position, get me on board, and the Italians, turn around again and take off for Italy across the stretch of the Adriatic. The strong fighter cover above made it to be a very simple, straightforward and safe operation, nothing to stop it in any form or shape. How could I make them see that?

I rushed for the survival kit again tore out another red Very cartridge, sending its shooting flame arcing out towards them. What in hell was holding them back?

Go into the sea again when I'd only just recovered from my gruelling immersion in it? Paddle out there in my dinghy two hundred yards? The Lord be with me!

Strongly, I knew I did not want to do it, fearful they would fly off without me, how long would they wait for me? I told the English speaking chap what was going on, a plea of honest emphasis, in my voice, "I must go out to the aeroplane in my dinghy. When they see me they will come down on the water. I tell them come in here take all you into the aeroplane. We fly back to Italy together in aeroplane. You'll be safe. Away from the Germans."

A fierce babbling followed soon as he'd told them. Everyone talking at once, the planes overhead circling. The Italians heard my message, showing signs of doubt, but I knew they'd accept it anyway. They had no choice with all that firepower above us. It was my rescue, there was no option for me, they had to accept that. Into the sea it had to be for me. I'd persuaded the Catalina crew they were doing a fine rescue job capturing these chaps.

They continued jabbering and shouting around me. 'Bugger this', I thought, that Catalina would not stay up there forever. Impatient to go I walked away from them down to the waters edge and stooped to push my dinghy back into the cruel sea again. The STSCO chap, their boss man, shouted at me above the engine noises, the English speaker translating for him. I looked up. Three of them had their rifles pointed at me.

"You no go," he yelled, "we no swim." He waved the flattened palm of his hand at me, barring the way. I stood up, aggressively, facing them. They were frightened and threatening but I knew they didn't have enough guts to stop me, challenging my right to rescue. I would bloody well swim out there if needs be. They advanced on me, forming a line so that I could not go into the water. Another dragged the dinghy up clear of the shoreline.

"No!" he said, shaking his head violently. "No go!"

Then I twigged it. These chaps were a lot more frightened of their German masters than the planes overhead and me. We almost cancelled one another out as a threat to them. They couldn't straf anything while I was there.

The Catalina started winking his message again. I caught something ending with 'TOMORROW'. The bastards were going to leave me! They were not going to come down. I couldn't believe it. I could not believe my rescue was almost within shouting distance but would leave me.

I saw them turn away and continue heading seaward in profound disbelief. This was certainly the most depressing sight of my life.

I waved my arms wildly as if to pull them back again, a futile gesture, the engine noise fading into the dismal horizon. The Spits were gone, I was alone, crushed in defeat. Why, oh why, had this happened to me? The sodden wetness of my clothes, the ghastly green stain of everything about me re-imposed my misery. I stood there depressed, lonely, forsaken. Was that message they had blinked out about trying again tomorrow? Would anything be different if they did have another go? It was too much to think about. Please God make it happen. Make them come back for me.

My efforts had been useless. Shock and fatigue came back; I was spent. Their spokesman chap tapped my shoulder, motioning we should go up to the top of the escarpment where they had their camp. I told him the Catalina would come back tomorrow. "Si, si," he nodded, unconvinced.

I stood, looking at the water, watching its slow surge up the bare rock, falling away and leaving its wet mark until the next wave came. Tired, lost and hungry I felt completely abandoned.

They shouted to me as I stood there. Turning, I saw three of them gesture commandingly; there was a different mood about them now. My hopes shattered, I started after them with the spokesman at my side, not speaking, labouring at the effort needed for the steep climb. My legs were like lead. I paused every few minutes to catch my breath. Going on seeing them above me, waiting, checking I was still moving in the right direction. Finally, scrambling through a small cleft I emerged out onto a neat plateau of flat earth, barren except for two huts, the position they used for their plane spotting activities and a well. I wondered if, from the air, these had the appearance of machine gun posts. I couldn't accept that the Catalina had gone away without some cause, some unknown reason for failing me in my hour of deliverance. Did the observer post, or the structure over the well look like a threat?

It was clear that the Italians didn't know what to do with me. I was an intruder, a foreigner in their midst, an alien that didn't fit. I wandered to the plateau lip, its sombre hues reflected in the water below, the gloom of the sweeping slopes of bare island all around me. The evening light was beginning to fade, making the landscape look even more depressing. Where was I now? Did the island have a hidden Partisan force? Was there a slightest chance I'd be rescued from the place? What could I do? My thoughts rushed around in bewildering circles trying to see a way out. Surely, I wondered, all was not lost yet. I wasn't their prisoner! They were only sheltering me?

Turning back into the small encampment I saw the NCO chap conferring with the English speaker and two others. Nothing in their incomprehensible Italian gabble, or their constant movement of hands in my direction, showed either friendliness or comfort for my wellbeing.

"Inglees! Inglees!" he called, "We eat food," pointing towards one of the huts, "we have some drink, you sleep." I went to where they indicated, very austere, just a bare board table a few chairs and a couple of mattress beds in the corner. The food was Spartan fare: coarse black bread, a piece of cheese and some cold pasta. I was hungry enough to welcome anything edible, even though my stomach revolted against the food as I swallowed.

Two of them, the NCO and the translator, sat with me, gobbling their portions greedily. No one spoke; it was almost embarrassingly quiet. My first experience of the days to come, my own isolation in a new world of silence and thought, a kind of displaced mental process, absorbing what was around me without the relief of verbal communication. They left me inside the hut and went out, commanding me to stay there. The exhaustion of the day settled on me like a damp wet blanket. I slumped in my own misery, despondent, still wet from the sea. The solid bread and the goat's cheese had been a passing distraction. Now what? Only my own world of nothingness. All that journeying across the world to get here to finish up like this. The fight wasn't over yet… or was it?

I wandered across the months and years, seeking consolation. My tearful departure from home, Suva, in the beloved Fiji islands, the first boat trip, all that seasickness, a pause in Auckland, New Zealand, on to Sydney for a long wait, without money, wondering if the whole contingent of us had been forgotten, the tramp ship down to Melbourne, across the rolling Australian Bight to Freemantle and Perth, a brief pause. Then the endless weeks sweeping down deep into the boisterous Indian Ocean, in shipping isolation, almost touching the freezing Antarctic, avoiding the submarine threat: Durban, South Africa, dreary days in the train labouring up into Rhodesia, the converted pig pens of initial training in Bulawayo, proudly drawing my first RAF uniform, the exhilaration of initial flying in Tiger Moths at Belvedere outside Salisbury, advancing on to Harvards at Cranborne, proudly sewing on my pilots wings. The wild celebrations, then back to Capetown, waiting impatiently in the stark bareness of the primitive personnel holding unit, forever waiting, boarding the sardine packed troopship via Freetown, Sierre Leone, to Liverpool, on our way to fighter squadrons in the real war. The anti climax of arriving in UK, with weeks waiting again, milling around, hundreds of other bored, would-be pilots in the reception centre at Bournemouth, shaken by the terrible sight of a first bombing raid, the tantalising sight of Focke Wolf 190s skip raiding overhead, a posting on to Ternhill for refresher flying in Masters. At last, into the world of real aeroplanes, the excitement of Tealing, Scotland, No 56 Operational Training Unit flying the all powerful Hurricane fighter. The crushing news at the end of it, a bottleneck in fighter pilots, being side-lined to fly trainee air gunners around the sky in spent Boulton Paul Defiants, Masters and Ansons at bleak Walney island, Barrow-in-Furness. My continuous and desperate fight to escape from the clutches of Flying Training Command into a front-line fighter squadron. Rewarded at last and the second operational flying training unit on Spitfires. The ultimate posting, overseas again, immediate replacements via Algiers, the Middle East Command, and Naples. Then, at last, two and a half years from the beginning, No 249 Squadron, my special family fighting force. First the clapped out Spitfire Mk.Vc, then the super Mustangs. Dear God what a journey! Brindisi, Salonika, back to Brindisi, Sorrento, the rest camp and back to base. Now, Cherso Island in the Adriatic Sea. Please God don't let my war end in this miserable hut of a place! If only some kind of magic wand were to hand – one wave and all would be well again. Desperately I wanted to fly and to fight in an aeroplane again, not sit in this dismal hole with this miserable group of quisling Italian soldiers.

The door burst inwards, four of them entered. I held my peace. The spokesman lifted his arms wide as if welcoming me back into the fold. I looked, open mouthed, wondering what in hell was coming now.

"Inglees… Si! Demani, tomorrow, we go down wait for aeroplane coming." Just like that. A dawn rescue, a good idea. Perhaps it could be possible before the Germans came. He said they might be here in the afternoon with supplies and checking up. The way he told it I was less than certain. Down on the foreshore, before the Catalina gave up, they had been bubbling with optimism. Now it sounded like a tale. I had to say 'OK by me' nodding my head in approval. Was there an alternative?

"It is good", he said, "tomorrow we go Italia, now we have drink?"

They produced two sizeable bottles and glasses, saying it was good vino, proffering the first for inspection, with pride, for me to drink.

Drink was not something I needed, but their expansive behaviour, which offered a way out from the misery of my predicament, prevailed. The glass in my hand became bottomless. I followed what they did with each filling up. Down they went, smoothly, warming me through, lifting my tiredness and depression, each one tasting better than the last. They showed me the second bottle insisting I try it, something special again for me, it was stronger smelling, a spirit. My troubles were seeping away.

Gradually my senses spun and whirled out of control. I drifted into a pleasing coma, I felt mellow towards them, not caring any more about anything, anywhere. What the hell! They were my friends, allies in the war. Not their fault the Germans forced them to work against our cause. They would help me get back to my Squadron. I showed them I was tired, wanted to have a sleep. It had been a very, very, long day.

They helped me to my feet, moving me on to one of the corner beds. It was all so pleasant. I hadn't a care in the world. I knew only I wanted to lie down and to sleep and sleep, damp wet, green-stained clothing, squelchy flying boots and all. They lowered me on to the blessed bed of rest and left me to it. I must have passed out into the bottomless oblivion I sought.

CHAPTER 13

Betrayed

Some unknown stretch of time on into the dark night I became aware of a harsh sounding disturbance in the room, boots crashing, voices raised across my semi consciousness, filtering through my dazed senses. Half rising to see what was going on, I felt pain shoot across my forehead, throbbing in my temples, a cruel reminder of the evening's excesses. What was in that stuff they gave me? Blinking, confused, I sat on the edge of the bed thinking to go out for a piss.

Was it time to get up, go down to meet the Catalina? Cupping my head in my hands, pressing back the pain, I saw shapes beginning to form in the room, great burly bodies filling the darkness, a pattern, a kind of menace not there before. Trying to blink away the uncertainty of it, a torch flashed, stabbing out the darkness, the beam slamming across my sensitive eyes. I clamped them tight shut against the pain, lifting an arm to shield against the light.

"Hey! What goes on? What are you doing?" I was alarmed at the aggression in front of me, blinking against the light, trying to focus. What was this all about? The answer came with brutal clarity. A strong hand gripped my wrist in vice like squeeze, pulling me to my feet, grunting a word I could not fathom, two, three, four times.

Instinctively I knew to stand still, not resisting. Another flashlight behind the person holding my arm caught us in its beam. It was not the Italians. I saw a Luger pistol pointing at my guts. There were two others behind him with machine pistols aimed at me. The unmistakable SS badge glinted in the light. This was a German officer backed by three armed soldiers, weapons at the ready, their blue steel barrels clear in their deadly message.

Speechless, I stared at them, completely bewildered. What was there to do or to say? I was already their prisoner of war.

Forcing my hands up onto my head, they subjected me to thorough German roughing-up, searching, groping over every square inch of me. Grabbing my specially prepared toilet kit, the officer squeezed the tube of toothpaste dry and disembowelled my cake of soap, as if to find some hidden secret within. Seeing nothing more sinister than ordinary toilet articles he threw the empty tube and the cut up cake of soap on to the bed. Even my blood chit with 'Ja Sam Britanski' boldly printed all over it, disappointed him. His hostility surprised me. Why so brutal? I thought. I bore them no malice, no evil intent. I was their prisoner of war, no possible threat in any way. He ordered me back onto the bed to lie prone. Through the rest of the sleepless night one of them stood guard within a few feet. Was I that much of a risk?

Exhaustion had its way and I dropped off again to wake as the first light of day showed through the hut door. A big German soldier complete with menacing machine pistol stood within touching distance. I showed him I had to have a piss outside. He called the under officer and out we went. It was my goodbye to the hut and the Italians. Bastards! Still, their own lives and future well-being were more important to them than my miserable hide.

The Germans marched me off without so much as a word to the Italians, standing there to see me go; no ceremony with these SS guys. We made our way down the winding path that dropped steeply from the plateau, in single file, the under officer up front, leading me to god-knows-where, the three stone-faced goons bringing up the rear, machine pistols at the ready. If they thought at all it didn't show on their expressionless faces. What was I anyway? Some kind of bloody criminal about to spring a surprise against all that deadly fire power? I might be a POW but I was still an officer and was supposed to be treated with respect under the Geneva Convention, not to be threatened by this kind of aggressive attitude.

Every sharp stone, every rut in the tumbling path seemed to find its way underfoot as I stumbled and slid along at their dictated pace.

Why, oh why! had I made that fatal decision to paddle for dry land. If I'd only stayed out there in the calmness of the Adriatic, paddling around in circles to stimulate warmth, the sea marker spreading its green/yellow pattern far and wide, they would have found me soon enough. I would have been home and dry now, telling another tale. What a bloody awful blunder; a panic mistake. That made two in the same day: the first was breaking away from my attack too soon, into the line of flak fire, giving the bastards a better chance of a deflection shot. Only one unlucky shell out of the thousands they'd poured into the sky at us. It took only one!

My thoughts wandered from defiance against my predicament to a feeling of despair. I felt the way I looked, a comic, forlorn sight; ridiculous, cold, depressed, spent, my dye-stained clothes still damp, my fleece lined flying boots wet inside and out. I was a clown, a comic figure, unkempt, sea stained, mouth dry, head throbbing, placing my feet with care, trying to avoid the worst stones and ruts, moving uncertainly over the slope downwards. Their alien hostility forced me into isolation. I was at a low ebb and vulnerable; cut off from everything and everyone I knew.

They didn't speak to one another, they couldn't speak to me. Peremptory movements of a threatening gun muzzle communicated anything they wanted to say. 'Keep going' – a wave of the machine pistol, 'onwards, down there', until we arrived at the shoreline. 'Out on to the double plank Jetty', another gun barrel wave – 'get into the boat, climb into the stern, sit right there on the seat, stay there'. All in complete silence, even between them I did it, subdued, thinking if only one of you would show a human expression, some slight gesture of understanding, some measure of speech between the four of you. 'Sure I am the prisoner of war, your enemy, a fighter pilot in the Royal Air Force, but are we not humans with feelings, our lives remote from the norm? The war is almost over now and you pigs are on the losing side. Why were we hating one another to death anyway? Even now, as your prisoner, I have no hatred for you, no bitterness, even while you all stand there, deadly machine pistols, loaded, ready to blast me off the earth if I threaten you in any way'. Then a sense of guilt crossed my mixed up mind, 'Yesterday I attacked you in my Mustang. I wasn't trying to kill any of you personally, just destroy and damage the E Boats in the Harbour. I know I might have killed some of you, without being killed myself, but now it was all different, with me on the shifty end of the deal'. I knew if I was up there now above this boat it would be a beautiful target and I would go for it all guns blazing, aiming as carefully and deliberately as I knew. Yet, I did not accept we had to hate one another, Surely

---

Telephone No.: GERRARD 9234
Trunk Calls and Telegraphic Address: "AIR MINISTRY," LONDON

P.424173/P.4.A.2.

AIR MINISTRY,
(Casualty Branch),
73-77 OXFORD STREET,
LONDON, W.I.

19 October, 1944.

Madam,

I am commanded by the Air Council to confirm the telegram in which you were notified that your husband, Flying Officer Dennis Percy Francis McCaig, Royal Air Force, is missing as the result of air operations on 8th October, 1944.

The telegraphic report from Air Force Headquarters, North Africa, states that the Mustang aircraft in which your husband was flying was hit by enemy fire and crashed at Polycastron, approximately 30 miles north-north-west of Salonika, Greece. Your husband baled out and landed at Megala Livadia, approximately 45 miles north west of Salonika.

If he is prisoner of war he should be able to communicate with you in due course. Meanwhile enquiries are being made through the International Red Cross Committee, and as soon as any definite news is received you will be at once informed.

/If

Mrs. D.P.F. McCaig,
Lansdowne,
Staddens Road,
Burham-on-Sea,
Somerset.

not when together like this. I didn't want their friendship. I didn't want warm embraces or anything crazy like that. Just a touch of human understanding.

Mixed up, isolated from my own world, the coolness of the still morning around us, fanning my green and salt dried hair, the launch engine beating out its chugging sound over the bay, I could not find hate in me for them. I knew I was apprehensive, scared of what they might do to me, but hate? No, I didn't hate them.

My confused thoughts rambled on, going round and round, no logic, not any kind of constructive thought. I was pitifully lonely, demoralised and damp. We were on our own, fully exposed, cutting a long bow line of rippling sea going away on either side, a strafing Mustang pilot's dream target, no flak, plenty of water splashes to show where the bullets were going! A dawn recce flight, same as I had confidently led yesterday, could be speeding towards us even now. I could be killed by my own kind. Yesterday I'd been abandoned by my own. Funny thing that!

Across the bay we moved in steady progress, coming to the same panoramic spread of mountains falling down into the sea, I'd seen through my Mustang windscreen the previous morning. The buildings and jetty were in a different perspective from sea level with more time to look as we approached. The E Boats secured there were scarred, nicked and splintered; damaged by the multiple strikes from our six point five machine guns. They were the hallmarks of some good shooting from us. Yes! I thought, and now one of the creators of those hallmarks is being brought to you by the SS!

The boat and jetty damage lifted my spirits, compensation for my misfortune, a sad, salt dried, green-stained apparition being paraded before my enemy. But they'd done a good job of patching up the wharf and two of the E Boats had put to sea. We might have shot them up a bit but the attack had not been successful; the gain was theirs. No one could hope to retrieve Mustang D-Delta from the bottom of the Adriatic Sea, its was gone forever.

The goon closest to me waved his gun barrel, signalling, 'get out of the boat, wait there.' Leaving the other three we marched up hill, along an empty street, the people still indoors, no human activity anywhere, no-one paying me any attention at all. Coming into the main square of drab town he gun-halted me outside the largest building, face to face with a monstrous banner featuring a huge black swastika on an aggressive scarlet background, disfiguring one complete side of the wall. It was my first encounter with the repulsive emblem of power that was arrogantly displayed wherever the Germans conquered. All my training over the years had taught me to hate this enemy symbol. Now, as I stood facing it, the thought uppermost in my mind was to escape if any opportunity offered the slightest chance of success.

Half pushing me through a side door, the machine pistol waved me down onto a wooden platform against the bare wall, no sign of life anywhere. The gun barrel said 'stay put' and left through another door. I was on my own. Time dragged in suspense, I was hungry. Would they give me some food, what would happen next? Uncertainty slowed the passing minutes.

A door banged open, shocking me from my day dreaming, in reflex action Jumping to my feet, standing to see a young German lieutenant, neatly dressed, militarily impressive against my unwashed, uncombed, dyed green scruffiness. He had me at instant disadvantage, looking me up and down without expression of any kind, his SS emblems clearly visible on collar and cap. Flipping an index finger, he commanded me to come, not speaking, returning through his door. I entered. He pointed to a chair. I knew to wait until he spoke first. In heavily accented English he said, "Sit down, there," keeping his finger by way of indication as though I might be too dumb to understand what was required. He remained standing on his side of the formidable desk between us, staring hard, intimidating, unwavering, a full ten seconds. I sat down cautiously, waiting, uncertain how to cope with this smooth looking character. What was he going to say?

"You will answer some questions" he said, a statement of fact, not a request. I said nothing, I didn't move, my stomach churning fit to show my fear of the situation.

"What is your name? I told him, spelling it out. Slowly he wrote it down. "What is your initials?" he wrote them down. "What is your rank?" I told him. Slowly he wrote that down. "What is your service number?" I gave it to him slowly, figure by figure. He wrote that down.

"Gut", he said, looking up, his expression softening, "You are a pilot flying in the Royal Air Force?" I did not answer, nothing to say, the silence between us threatened, staring hard at one another. I gave way first,

"I will give you my number, rank and my name, I will not answer any other questions." He looked unmoved by my statement, nodding acknowledgement, surveying this thing in dirty clothes on the other side of his office desk. To my complete surprise he said "Gut, Flight Lieutenant, I do not ask you more questions. You can be taken away, You can go with the guard." The anticlimax of my interview completely floored me. I was almost willing to tell what he had wanted to know but kept my silence. He walked to the door, bellowed an order, calling a guard, I was dismissed. Was that all it was going to be? I wondered. The guard waved a beckoning hand at me, 'Kommen', he ordered and led me out into the passage way again. Along the corridor, he steered me, pointing to a flight of stone steps leading down into a cellar cum dungeon, three quarters below ground level. He gave me a little push through the iron door, slammed it shut, rasping the locking bolts home.

I found myself in a small square cell with whitewashed walls and a single window showing thin shafts of daylight through its four solid iron bars. A two-tier bunk lined one wall, straw-filled palliasses upon it; no blankets of any type. A bucket stinking strongly of stale urine occupied one corner. Graphic scratchings were marked into one wall: each horrible group measuring the passing of time, single strokes, grouped in sevens, struck through diagonally to mark days of the week, all ending with either a matchstick figure hanging by the neck from gallows or being shot against a wall. I counted thirty-seven horrible reminders left by those who had occupied the cell before me. Surely they would never execute me? The Germans were a civilised enemy, thorough, very disciplined. They would never do anything to me without some kind of trial in a court of military law. But then again, I knew it would be possible to rub someone like me out. No one would ever know how or where I'd disappeared. The sight of those sad etchings on the wall, fascinating at first, nagged at me, eroding what I had left of a vanishing courage. Oh, for the sound of other humans, I thought, my isolation heavy and forlorn; no noises, no voices, even in the distance, only an overwhelming quiet and the vile smell of the place.

No food came that day. In the late afternoon I could just detect the fading light outside, my cell darkening slowly until the blackness of night clamped down around me. I peed into the bucket, the noise sounding overloud in my ears, a puny challenge to the silence. I climbed to the top bunk of the tier, the hardness, the crackling crispness of straw sounding with my every move. At least, I thought, with German thoroughness there would be no bed bugs here. Shielded from the disturbing etchings on to the walls, in complete darkness, I slipped into blessed sleep.

The rasping bolts, crashing open, shattered my peace. The guard gestured, ordering me out, signing I must follow him. We climbed three flights of stairs higher into the building, seeing the light of day coming up with shafts of sunlight brightening the windows. He paused, knocking at the door, waiting. It opened revealing an older officer, the major, a boss man in charge of the town. Dismissing my guard he waved a hand at me.

"Come in, Flight Lieutenant." He spoke in flawless English. "Sit down there. You would like some coffee, a slice of bread. Ersatz but the best we have. I have heard your story and want to talk to you before you are taken off on your journey to prison camp in Germany."

The coffee was hot and very bitter. I ate the two slices of black bread he gave me with it, restraining an impulse to gobble it in one swift go. I didn't care if it was made of wood or not – I was hungry.

I felt embarrassment at being in his office, taking his hospitality, wondering what this was leading to, what I would be asked in return. It turned out that his concern was about the end of the war. "It cannot be long now?" he said as if I had the full answer. "Then we must face the Bolsheviks. Both countries, Germany and England. They will come this way?" I looked at him blankly, no idea where they would come or how. No concern of mine. The only communists I'd seen were in Greece waiting in the sidelines to seize power, soon as the Germans pulled out. Maybe he was right but I was not for telling him.

"Thank you for my breakfast Major," I said, "I was very hungry. I have had no food for two days. I cannot tell you about the communists." Shaking my head, "I do not know these things they are political. I am only a pilot in the Royal Air Force." He knew that anyway.

My answer opened a floodgate for his views. He stood up, pacing restlessly around his office space, launching into details about Russian atrocities, their overwhelming masses, their insatiable greed to conquer all Europe and rule it with the same kind of ruthless terrorism being practised now as they advanced into central Europe. I had very little idea of what he was talking about, saying nothing, just listening, wondering when it would stop, what was I supposed to say in response? He finished speaking almost as abruptly as he'd started.

"You should not have been given the criminal cell last night. You are not a criminal. A prisoner of war, an officer. You will have a room for now. Tomorrow you go to Trieste. They will take you to Germany."

That was it. He dismissed me, calling the guard. It was confusing. I went from his office thankful to get out, away from him, thankful for his food and drink and a better place to stay than the intimidating and stinking underground cell.

The room was bare, just a bed covered in blankets, with one small window looking out onto an orchard. He shut the door, locking it for security and walked away down the passage. Silence and isolation surrounded me. The window showed me nothing, only fruit trees and long grass.

I had read how prisoners placed in solitary maintained their sanity doing whatever was possible with whatever was available. Round and round the room I walked counting the steps going for a long distance. One thousand seven hundred and sixty yards in a mile. Counting, counting, counting across the minutes and the hours with nothing more to measure the time than the changing patterns of sunlight. It helped.

In the fading twilight my door was unlocked, the guard entered and placed a hunk of black bread and a bowl of soup on the bed. He said nothing and left, locking the door again, retreating down the passage.

I ate it all. The soup was good and the bread a real chewers challenge but it was food. When he returned I would tell him I wanted a piss.

From my earliest days as the son of a colonial officer working in the remote districts of Fiji, I had been forced to find my own pleasures; other children, other diversions were something rare to be enjoyed. I had grown up to be a loner, without companions until I went to boarding school away from home. It stood me in good stead now that I was being forced to pass the time without any stimulation of any kind. It was hard going. I recited poetry, then prayers, then more walking around the room. If only one human being had appeared in the orchard it would have been a huge bonus, a counterbalance to my isolation. When it got dark I lay down and concentrated on sleep. At least my clothes had dried out and the fleecy lining of my flying boots was only damp. I took them off.

CHAPTER 14

A Long Trek Begins

My door lock clicked open loudly, shattering the peace of sleep. It was still dark but getting light. I had no idea how long I had slept, maybe ten hours. A new face entered the room, machine pistol at the ready. He waved me to come out and to move down the passage. I stopped, showing I had to have a piss. We went on after that, outside to a waiting car. He bundled me into the back, climbed in beside me, a great fat arsed brute whose size pushed me hard against my side of the car. A lieutenant and the driver occupied the front seats as we drove off without a word.

My guard placed the machine pistol between his thighs as if to warn me. We took a winding road out of the town square for the first hour, the sun beginning to light up the day, stirring the swirling fog around us, forcing the driver to crawl along with blinkered headlights on. At least this was more entertaining than my room of isolation and although I recognised the three with me as the enemy, at least they were human companions, albeit very silent ones, stone-faced goons with guns. We joined some kind of main highway carved into the hillside above the coastline. It was a splendid scenic drive, a sheer drop all the way down to the water. I watched the mists over a calm sea below gradually burning off. Each curve in the road brought something new to see before winding back in land. The beauty of our drive went on for hours, long enough to feel my bum going numb on the hardness of the seat.

They stopped the car at a mountain stream, about midday, giving me a piece of bread and a chunk of sausage, a meagre ration but more welcome than I was willing to show, I hadn't eaten since the bowl of soup with black bread last night. They nodded that I could take a piss in the stream that was cascading under the road, watching me closely.

Back into our drive again my mind wandered from looking at the scenery, thinking about my impending journey to a POW camp, right up into Germany, a hell of a long way from here. Above all else, I had to keep alert, look for a chance to escape, nothing too risky though, the war was too near the end for that, I had no death wish. Where would I go anyway? South to the allied advance up the Italian peninsular, lie low in some sympathetic farm? I had little idea other than to stay alive. Perhaps the armies advancing rapidly through France towards Germany would be the best bet. A stupid fantasy, that was miles away, better to sit tight for now and see what developed.

The hours of monotonous driving took us into the darkening of evening and the outskirts of a big town. We stopped outside a formidable looking place and they ordered me out. My guard made his bid and was granted entrance with me. It was a bloody prison. I couldn't believe it. What were they doing? Whatever it was there was no finding out.

"What in hell are you doing with me?" I blustered, "I am a British officer, not a bloody criminal!" My guard looked at me while I spoke, not understanding one solitary word. He checked me in, signing some kind of register, and a warder took my arm forcibly until I shook him off, leading me up two flights of stairs to an empty cell, pushing me in, clanking the open grill doors shut and locking it. The place was like a monkey cage; a bare room with a filthy looking bed and a lavatory opening in one corner. Shouting, whistling and clonking was going on all around. I was outraged beyond belief. What was this all about? I could only imagine they had secured me here overnight for want of a better place. I sure hoped so.

Sleep was difficult with some ape making a noise throughout the night, but sleep I did, in snatches.

I was almost pleased to see my guard in the early morning, to get out of this repulsive madhouse. He did not speak when the warder handed me over but looked almost sympathetic. We walked off into a drizzling rain going for about half an hour, reaching a staging post with more big diesel trucks than I'd ever seen before. He checked me in, clearing my presence to be there, took me to one of the trucks, ordered me up on top of the lumpy containers piled high inside, replacing and securing the heavy canvas canopy over the back. 'No way out of that,' I thought. It was cold, dark and clammy damp. I knew they were taking me somewhere but where that might be was a complete mystery. I tried to make the most of it, heaving and burrowing away at the loose shaped containers, seeking some warmth. I slept until disturbed by the vibrating start up of the lorry. We were off, gears grinding, slow moving, must be a convoy, I thought. I stayed still comfortable enough to be there while there was no choice, no way out. 'What a bloody miserable turn up,' I thought.

Bouncing with the movement of the truck, half-asleep, half-cold, I heard the thrumming of aeroplane engines high above the truck's diesel noise. Another passing plane on its way somewhere. How I longed to fly again.

The noise increased in volume, more planes, low down, overhead, a concentration, a raid of some kind and nearby by the sound of it. Wide-awake and wondering, I heard the first bombs crash and explode, very close, pressure waves hitting the side of the truck. The blasts became louder and louder, each huge sound eclipsed the last one. All hell was breaking loose out there. I burrowed deeper into my funk hole, hiding within the security of it. It saved my life. The next tearing eruption was almost on top of us. The truck's canvas canopy swooshed away into the darkness, sucking a terrifying wave of air across the top of my position. It ripped the world around us apart, revealing vivid flashes of blinding light, another and another, the whole countryside visible, our convoy, exposed naked by parachute flares. They were bombing the nearby town, it was illuminated as bright as day.

I peered out from my position deep within the bundles filling the truck, shaken by the lethal forces at work in the world around us. I couldn't think what to do. Each explosion compressed the air and sucked it away, stopping the truck in confusion. It veered over heavily to one side, nowhere to hide. I was scared stiff by the chaos, the and noise and the certain knowledge that I was about to be killed by my own forces. I had to escape before the next one landed on top of me.

Without thinking clearly, just not wanting to be killed in this way, wanting to be out in the open, away from the any tangled debris of our motor truck I jumped blindly from high up above the tailboard. Crashing painfully onto the road I rolled down into a drain filled with water and mud. Thank God nothing felt broken, I could move my arms and legs. I felt safer down here, watching every explosion away across the road.

They were after the town, shattering and tearing its heart out, the buildings outlined with each lurid eruption. They bombed in some kind of racetrack pattern with deadly intent, one after the other, each plane sounding overhead, moving on to target, releasing its devastating load, flying away, followed by yet more terrible missions of death.

I suddenly realised this was my moment to escape. No sign of any soldiery anywhere, only the line of trucks clearly visible in the false light. Carefully feeling my way, groping in front, arms straight out ahead I moved along the wet slippery bank, feet splashing in a few inches of water, waiting for each bomb illumination to light my way, my heart racing at a thousand revs. I made out the dark shape of a large culvert, the drain turning to pass at right angles under the roadway. It afforded a good opportunity to shelter from the chaos outside; I felt too close to the convoy. I decided to wait in this shelter for the raid to stop. The flares were already reaching the ground, going out, giving the night back its darkness. A bank parallel to the centre stream went through to the far end. Another flash of shattering light from the bombs. It looked good. They'd never know to look for me in here, never find me in the dark.

Those bastards up there were our aircraft. The raid had given me the chance to make a break. I hadn't been killed, I might make it yet, worth a try, I might find a friendly Italian family out in the country willing to give me shelter. I felt better, unsure but with enough courage to go on, to escape, please God.

The pandemonium of the bomber raid tailed off, the flares died down, the security of night returned, a faint glow, a burst of colour here and there, distant flickering fires where destruction from the bombs still stayed alive. The droning sound of engines passed out of earshot followed by strange quietness. I had to move on before they started looking, searching me out.

Blindly, on all fours, I edged through the culvert, going cautiously to the far end, all senses alert to the darkness and my purpose of escaping from the convoy. I bumped into a strangely silent body of people before I knew they were there – others who had had the same idea of sheltering from the air raid. Muted by the turmoil above, they were sitting, waiting for the time to emerge again. A torch flashed into my eyes, sweeping up and down to get a clearer identification of the intruder.

"Halt!" came the shout from the darkness. I stopped dead, guessing that I had blundered into some German soldiers from the convoy who were reluctant to make a move before they judged it to be safe again. Damn and blast! Having summoned the will to escape, it was over, over before it had started. Two of them arrived with the flashlight, recognising me, gabbling away to each other, probably deciding they had secured me. They accepted my presence with no further challenge or threat, taking me into their custody. We had no way of communicating. I could only think that they decided I had done no more than mirror their own self-preservation instincts in seeking a safety shelter under the culvert.

We went up onto the roadway collecting together, measuring the damage to the convoy. I stood listening to their talk, seeing myself pointed out as one of the problems to be settled. Two trucks were abandoned, damaged during the air raid. They loaded me into the back of another with a guard, gun barrel indicating where I must sit. The convoy restarted, lumbering away into the night, gradually winding uphill into the mountains, zig-zagging through the hairpin bends, crashing through the gears as the gradients steepened. Slowly the change in temperature seeped into me. I saw signs of the snowline receding away behind us as we climbed.

Tired and hungry, I could not have cared less about anybody or any bloody thing.

The whole idea of making a break for it left my mind. On we crawled in low gear, the rear of the truck swinging around each hairpin bend, changing down, changing up in audible metal crashes in the gear box, the engine racing, winding up revs with each change, the jarring bumps and jumps from the road surface stabbing through into my body.

We stopped. My original escort appeared, motioning me down into the just visible dawning of daylight. We marched off on to a branch road making for open ground that looked like an airfield. With no idea where in the world we might be, I tried the primitive communication of sign language. My guard, rifle slung casually across his back, had no idea what I was getting at. He shrugged his shoulders, motioning me to go on, showing he too exhausted by the horrors we had both come through in the night. We passed through a guarded gate, to be directed to a building some distance down the road. It was an airfield with misty outlines of planes I could recognise parked, picketed, engine cowlings covered up. I was being put into the hands of the Luftwaffe. Maybe they'd fly me up into Germany. Another truck ride like that and I'd cut my throat!

I was taken into a large open room, directed to one corner and shown to sit and wait. Waiting, isolated from the opportunity to speak, was now a norm in my life. To my complete surprise they brought me a cup of hot ersatz coffee and a hunk of black bread, a real delight, a feast of pleasure. An English-speaking corporal arrived, told me I must wait 'here' while they found me an escort. He would take me into Germany. The man was returning from duty.

"Where am I now?" encouraged by the opportunity, thinking he wasn't going to tell me that.

"Ah yes!" he said, seeming to understand I had a right know, "this is Villach, you will go by train from here," That was all. No more conversation. He left and I sat, closing my eyes, nodding off, head jerking straight, fighting off my overwhelming weariness. I slept in snatches.

The noise level built up around me, Luftwaffe uniforms going to and fro, ignoring my presence. Midday came and with it another thick slice of black bread and a piece of very edible sausage, more food than I'd been given for days.

So I was in or near Villach, with only the slightest idea where Villach might be and whether it was hours or days from where I was being taken. Yet for the first time since capture I felt confident about my safety, satisfied for the moment I was in one piece. I sensed no hostility in this place, not even curiosity about my being there. Looking myself over I was still in a stained green state, mud from last night covering my flying boots and trouser knees. I felt dirty all over, not a pleasant sight I was sure and I couldn't see all of it. I had not washed, my hair had not been combed for days, my teeth felt like sandpaper. What a bloody sight!

About mid afternoon a pleasant looking under officer approach, carrying a rifle over his shoulder, a knapsack on his back, handing me a parcel without speaking. It contained some four inches of sausage and a large lump of black bread. What for? My expression asked the question.

"You keep," he said, "we go." Just like that, his hand gesturing towards the door, to some unknown destination beyond. No introduction, no explanation, just 'we go'. I showed him I wanted to wash and have a piss. He took me into an austere ablution hut and stood watching. I had no towel or mirror, doing the best I could manage. It felt better anyway, enough to ask him "Where am I going? the question was inevitable. Gun or no gun I had a right to know at least that. He accepted.

"Train, tonight, we go to Germany." Thank goodness he spoke some words of English, albeit reluctantly and heavily accented.

We walked an endless distance from the airfield into a dark and overcast evening, reaching a rail siding.

He appeared to know what be was doing, finding a train guard, showing papers and boarding a hard-seated passenger carriage, already loaded with a mixture of people sitting quietly, waiting to go somewhere. He showed me where to sit, wedging ourselves between bodies already there. They grunted and shifted to give us enough space.

I recognised that trains moved only by night; anything on the road or rail in daylight was an inviting target to the same kind of marauding fighters missions I had flown all over the Balkans. A familiar hissing of steam up front indicated we'd soon roll. I sat, not daring to move, not knowing whether those around recognised me for what I was, not knowing whether they were friendly or hostile. Wedged between them, against an outside wall, I felt a welcome level of body generated warmth.

Our long train jerked into movement, hissing and steaming through the night. I slept in fits and starts, accepting my level of discomfort as better than my previous journeys. All I had to do was sit there. To my surprise, when daylight came we kept going. The tired-looking passengers around me unwrapped packages of food: bread and sausage mostly, cheese here and there. I did the same, eating self-consciously, preserving my scarce supply. We stopped at regular intervals; some got off, others boarded. It went on until midday. On an open pine-wooded stretch we came to a brake screeching halt, the engine bursting out several short sharp whistles. Above the shrilling noise of the whistle I heard the threatening sound of diving planes and the fearsome chatter of machine guns coming down on us. I couldn't see anything, guessing by the sound that they were strafing along the train, going for the locomotive, two of them making one quick diving pass. I heard the rattling of multiple guns as they paused overhead, then silence. I heard screams down the carriages, our compartment moving around panicking, shouting, pandemonium. It had all been very quick and confusing, now the fighters had gone. I was untouched, thank God.

Everyone around me had a look of relief, they too were untouched, shaken to an extreme but we had taken no hits, the multiple explosions following each burst of gunfire, striking and bursting on either side of our carriage had been terrifying but no physical harm done in our carriage.

Gradually the fear, the fever pitch of excitement subsided and the passengers around us quietened down to a soft babbling. I wondered if they would find a source of revenge in recognising me. Nothing happened.

The loco whistled a couple of shrill blasts, waited until the paniced passengers reboarded and slowly jerked into movement again. The fighters had missed him this time. I'd never know what success they had down behind us.

Later in the day we steamed slowly into a large station and looking out I saw British POWs working on the track, reawakening my mind to escape. I wondered if they could help with a way to go. Waving a hand I called, "Hello there, You chaps British?" They turned away, ignoring me, shovelling at the heavy gravel between the sleepers. My escort grabbed at my arm. We walked a mile or so to a Luftwaffe encampment, an airfield with a few ME109s and FW190s parked on the perimeter. If only I'd had a chance at that lot, I thought, before being ushered inside some sort of aircrew Mess. The pilots were courteous, making sure I was comfortable, they sat me down and gave me a beer: real World War I stuff, comrades in a common line of business and all that. The meal they gave me was excellent, even some small-talk about flying; nothing important for fear of disclosing information to the enemy, reserved, but almost friendly. I felt out of place given my appearance compared with the neatness of their uniforms.

My escort came for me again in the early evening, another railway station, another journey through the night, even more packed in than the previous leg. Finally, we came to a stop out in the blue, no town, no station, just the railway paralleled by a broad road. It was a mass exodus – everybody out. Looking out along the line I saw a milling mass getting out, a mixture of uniforms and civilians, men, women and children, all with a common purpose as if they knew what was happening. My escort pointed and I went to alight with everybody else. We must walk the rest of the way to our destination.

He motioned me along. I cocked my head, spread my hands in query, wanting to know what was what. He pointed along the line saying, "We go," which seemed bloody obvious to me. I wanted to know where 'we go' and why we were going there on foot with the large moving mob from the train. He looked as if weighing up what to tell me, and how. We had not spoken above a few words in the days and nights travelled together, his normal pattern of communication a variety of signs, nods of his head and expressions of face – not to mention my intelligent interpretations of them – but we'd formed a strange kind of rapport.

"Night before, bombers come – bomb town. Boomf! Plenty damage, plenty peoples. Train no go. We walk round Aschaffenburg, train other side." I was amazed at his command of English and the length of his explanation, each part of it emphasised with hands and face, getting the message across. He hadn't finished yet, perhaps the real reason for his launching into the English language and in such detail. "You no noise – no talk – close me – peoples very angry – kill you."

The last bit struck home, worrying me. I'd wondered throughout the long dreary journey about being recognised, being vulnerable to anyone wanting to have a go, hating the enemy they saw in me. He hitched his gun again and pointed the way, absorbing us in the general mass of quietly walking people. So, at long last I knew we had arrived at a known destination. But where in hell was Aschaffenburg? Somewhere in about mid Germany I reckoned. We'd been going so long without any of the customary breaks for food or drink, only daylight and darkness, that I had lost all sense of time. We were there now, it was early morning, the town licking its wounds from overnight bombing, suffering what he said, heavy damage and loss of human life.

We found a soup kitchen out in the open. A huge cauldron surrounded by people waiting to get a share. Well disciplined, no one pushing or shoving. Food! I thought – I would do a lot for some of that. It smelled good. My meagre lump of bread and sausage, long since gone. He joined the end of a line, showing me to stay put. I wasn't about to run away from this one and in this place, trying to look as inconspicuous as possible, knowing my green stained clothing was very different from the sombre browns and blacks around me.

When he returned with two good sized bowls and spoons, I could have kissed him! I was ravenous. It tasted delicious in flavour, full of substance, a happy reviver of spirits, nothing had ever tasted like that anywhere in the world. I stood enjoying the feeling it gave while he returned the bowls and spoons, wondering if we were to go on now to who knew where.

CHAPTER 15

Companionship & Compassion

A pair came up to us. Another guard with an American prisoner, a Flying Fortress air gunner, he said. Marvellous! Some one to talk to in English. We greeted one another in a mood of common sympathy. Two complete strangers from two completely different worlds of life and flying. For a moment we stood shyly looking one another, testing for rapport. In lowered voice, as though some one might overhear our flying secrets, we exchanged experiences. Where we'd come from, what we were flying, how we'd been shot down, where and then how we had got right here to Aschaffenburg. So! Where were we going from here? Neither of us knew. His escort spoke less English than mine.

We agreed it would be too bloody dangerous trying to take off, trying to escape now. He looked to see if I agreed, telling me he'd had a real hard parachute landing, something in his lower back, very painful. When I asked about the rest of his crew he shook his head sadly. The Fort had almost disintegrated from a direct hit. I wanted to raise his spirits, forget about my own situation waiting for his bowl of hot soup, the big reviver. We talked quietly, watching our escorts do the same thing. I hoped they'd be working on how we might avoid attention, there were real dangers from local hostility if we were recognised as allied aircrew. His clothes were more military and conspicuous than mine. I asked him to take off his cap, to put it in his pocket.

"Gut," they said motioning we must now skirt the town, keeping out in the direction of his waving hand. We went, the American limping, they followed close. There was destruction and rubble everywhere, a torn and jumbled mass of bricks and wood and plaster, some still smouldering, people digging at it, searching for what only they knew to be there. A large group stopped working, looking up at us, quickly spotting who we were. Some of them detached, following us. We quickened our pace. They called to our guards, getting very little in response, the words unintelligible, the tone of voice unmistakable, sounding in shouted anger. They knew who we were and they were after us. Exposed and vulnerable, frightened by the sudden turn of events, we continued on, heads down, as if to hide ourselves in the open. Another group ahead blocked our way, cornering the four of us against a half-demolished brick wall. We all turned to face them, our two guards slightly in front to fend off, indicating they wanted no trouble. Keep it calm, holding palms down as if to suppress the growing anger advancing on us.

A large jagged rock flew through the air between the guards, missing us. Then a second smashed into the American kid's eye making a mushy dull sort of sound. A crunch of flesh and bone. He went down on his knees, in the dust and more stones rained about us, not striking home with any force. I knelt to help him. The angry mob's success seemed to silence them for the moment. Our two guards stirred into action at the sight of blood spurting, seeing we'd been damaged. They unslung their guns, warning anybody not to come closer, to stop throwing. I bent down, lifting the kid's head, wanting to staunch the blood coming from his eyebrow, streaming down his face. He looked a mess, surprised and terrified at what they had done to him. He gave a pleading look to be left alone. He meant them no harm. Fortunately for us, they were not a blood-lust mob, merely people frustrated and angry at what the bombers had done to them. They held off. The kid's guard pulled a field dressing from his knapsack, wrapping it skilfully around the lad's head as the locals watched.

We left them to their excavation tasks, moving on. Two arrogant looking youths in uniform, in their early teens, let us come up to them, one spitting a mouthful of filthy saliva down the side of my face. I recoiled in horror, wiping it away on my sleeve, wanting to take a swipe at him. My escort chap intervened, pushing the lad aside, saying something I could not know. We kept going, trying to ignore anyone in sight, bruised by the encounters, shaken. We knew they had been harmed, but not by us. We'd walked about an hour, going slowly, matching the American's limping progress, not speaking. A German civilian hailed our guards, speaking words, seeming to challenge our progress. My chap turned to me, asking, "You want eat food. Man's house place?" I looked at the American.

"This chap is asking us to go to his house and have some of his food. Could be a trap. What do you think?"

"Sure, bud. If its OK by you, its OK by me. These two guards will take care of us. Nothing to fear here. Lets go."

They side-tracked us to a comfortable looking farmhouse, took us in, redressed his wound, sitting us at a central table, covered with a lace cloth, placing plates of soup before us with a small loaf of black bread. It was a feast. We ate self consciously and greedily, not believing our good fortune after the morning's incidents. We could not speak to our generous hosts, we could not ask them why they had been so wondrously kind. We could only say thank you, in English, showing heartfelt signs. They brought us photographs of young boys in uniform, apparently their sons. We made appropriate noises and signs of understanding, frustrated at not being able to talk about our miraculous experience with them.

My escort indicated we must go. More important things to do than sitting in relative comfort, stomachs content again, talking without words. He made no effort to interpret. Nothing could spoil that wonder meal, the sheer joy of Christian charity from these two elderly Germans. The mother made a last minute inspection of the kid's wound, waving hands, showing all was well, as best we could expect. We shook hands in farewell, grinning our gratitude, our deep appreciation for what they had done, then off again feeling human, fortified against the further encounters to come.

Nothing happened in the miles we walked to the other side of the town, finding a train, in steam, almost waiting for us to get there.

Our journey proved the first of many, packed tight with other travelling human beings, drab, tired looking, indifferent to their surroundings, enduring what they must do to get wherever they were going. A picture of the terrors of war, the constant allied air attacks, the total disruption to normal lives reflected in many faces around us. Together we were on the receiving end of a monstrous tragedy. There was nothing to fear in them. Even the uniforms scattered in the mix of bodies showed despondency, a kind of obedient automation, doing what they had to do.

Each train leg was a pattern of scrambling down, getting off, walking around the destroyed area, travelling the next unknown distance, to the next stage, to the next serviceable piece of line or waiting locomotive and its line of Spartan carriages. Sometimes we sat, sometimes we stood, sometimes we squatted, legs to heavy to support us all the way. Closely wedged together, less conspicuous, only occasionally drawing attention, a harsh word fended off by our guards. Ironically, as well as being our captors, they were our protection against their own people. Any measure of time or direction of travel faded with the passing hours. We hung together, exhausted, moving in a kind of layered consciousness, night and day and the passing of time between.

We did what our guards said, accepting the situation in a detached way, no real feelings, no hunger, no nothing. For all we knew there could have been much doubling over circuitous routes, it mattered not, they were taking us to an allied POW camp. Our judgement was that we were better off to stay with them until we got there in one piece, through this hostile land, their guns the only insurance of our safety along the way.

At Frankfurt main station, awaiting yet another connection of trains, they made us understand they wanted our word not to try and escape. To where? I thought. How? The kid said OK. If they wanted to go off and come back it was OK by him. I nodded agreement. Not really a choice.

They took us deep into the station cellars, bare, cold, damp, concrete slabs placed around the dripping walls, no light. Huge rats moved evilly, sniffing their way, skulking in the depths of darkness. We wondered if the guards would ever come back, much easier to leave us here than worry about the rest of the journey. The kid's spirits had risen with their departure.

"Listen!" he shouted into the dark cavernous space, his voice echoing and bouncing around us, "if any of you goddam rats come any closer, I'll damn well eat you." I looked at him and we both laughed. It broke up the eerie silence of the place.

I lay down on one of the big concrete slabs feeling the coldness of it through my battledress top, half-dozing. We were alerted by voices, English speaking voices, American accents. Five of them came down the steps, pausing at the sight of us, their clothes torn and scorched, two had their heads wrapped in soiled bandages, the brown stain of dried blood showing through. They were a sorry sight, bedraggled, heavy with fatigue. I thought to break the silence, "HI there! How ya doing? We're a couple of captured flyers. He's a Fort air gunner, I'm a British fighter pilot. How long have you been on the go?" They moved towards us cautiously seeming to welcome the exchange.

"Hi! We were knocked down a few nights ago. Our goons wanted a break. They've gone off. We promised to stay put. No place to go." He shrugged his shoulders, hands uppermost, chuckling at his own half joke. We were shot up, caught fire and had to go out. They were waiting for us on the ground, took us to a hospital, patched us up a bit, gave us some food. They were Germans, but we had good treatment."

"Goes for us too." I said.

Close up, their condition was almost too much to see. Three faces taught with bright red skin, visibly burnt showing scarlet covered flesh tissue, no sign of hair anywhere, one of them even had the tops of his ears burnt away. I realised that my experiences were very small beer compared to what they had suffered. The three of them must certainly have been in a great deal of pain and yet their spirits were high. We relaxed with one another, no need to play it secretly, they were very obviously part of a Fort bomber crew and willing to swap stories in a quiet easy way, relishing their heavy daylight bombing raids of German cities.

"Man! you should have seen that place burn." No question of feeling sorry for the personal outcome to each of them. "You Britishers did it at night we followed up next day. Must have been one hell of a place to be down there. Why don't the bastards give in? They've lost. They must know it." His companions tried slowing his excitement down, "Steady Al. We're alive, and boy, that's enough for me!" We talked on, seeking some comfort from one another's plight. They had the kind of optimistic guts that would inspire anyone.

Our two guards returned, looking pleased with their venture. They had not deserted us after all. There was no exchange between us, only a gesturing we must go. I could not leave without saying something to the Yanks,

"Goodbye, you chaps. I hope it goes well with you. God bless you." It sounded formal but I knew nothing else to say.

The next of our train legs stretched out into another sleepless night on hard seats, dozing, jerking awake, wondering where to this time.

In first light we were turned out, alighting to see a whole gaggle of British, Americans and a few other odds and sods, grouped together, travelling the same as us. My guard disappeared; I lost sight of the Yank. Funny, we had, all four of us, travelled through countless hours together and then whoosh, they were all gone. Who cared anyway, my sole concern now was my own survival.

Several German guards milled around, placing us into three orderly ranks, motioning we should go in file. It was a long walk up a hill until at the top our column entered the fastness of my first barbed wire enclosure, an interrogation centre somewhere in Germany.

CHAPTER 16

Interrogation

We were split up into small groups, taken into bare rooms with nothing but a wooden wall seat; no one talked. This was the time to be guarded. Training sessions had emphasised the tricks that may be used to get information: some intimidating, some bluff. "They are very good at it, but all you have to do under the Geneva Convention, is give your number, rank and name." What could they want from me anyway? The war was nearly over – nothing to fear from this lot. I sat with my thoughts, silently speculating about what was coming next. Sitting, waiting, worrying, hoping something would happen soon. Maybe this was part of the softening-up process; leave them alone long enough they would talk. Was the place bugged?

The routine started as a welcome relief, better than sitting in a vacuum, visualising the worst. Photographs, fingerprinting, in orderly sequence, no words spoken, number, rank, name, entered on the identification card then into a lone cell waiting for interrogation. I lay back on the hard straw sack, pleased to rest, sensing a routine – switching the heating system on and off. Was it faulty; was it deliberate? First too hot then slowly getting colder until it was really cold for a full half-hour. On again with the heat, stifling hot. If the sequence was deliberate, meant to do something, it failed with me, it was no more than passing discomfort. Bugger them!

At OTU they had said, "Above all, stay calm, don't get heated up." Heated up? I thought, what a joke. "Remember don't say anything at all, not a word. Don't let them get you going, they will want you to talk, using your family, anything. Before you know it you will be gabbling away. That's when you are vulnerable, wide open, at their mercy, they know it. Number, rank and name, that's all."

The Germans were very thorough, their staff at interrogation centres, highly trained. Who would know anyway if I disappeared from the face of the earth? Round and round went my tortured mind, full of tired daydreams, alone in my empty cell, a repeated pattern of disjointed, hazy thinking, fostering insecurity. Why this routine anyway?

I heard a scuffling noise outside my door, almost a relief sound from the silence and the changing temperatures. Someone had slid a plate of thin soup and a half slice of black bread under my door.

Should I eat? Would they know if I left it? Would they guess at my resistance? I ate it anyway; I was very, very hungry.

Around dusk a tapping on my door startled me into the present. I'd dozed and woken, wondering where I was. Another bowl of soup some more dried bread. There were still human beings out there somewhere, they'd even remembered I was in here, alive. The food was more than I'd enjoyed during those nights and days of my train journeys.

All through my captured days and nights, being alone, without any sound of others was my greatest difficulty. I was not a strong survivor of the isolation treatment, my mind seemed to wander of its own free will, across fields of fantasy if there was nothing left to focus on, or to distract me. I was not sure whether I would come to any harm. Would they employ techniques of persuasion, beyond my capacity to resist? Would they shoot me; or starve me?

On my second day of incarceration, as I wondered how long this would go on, another plate appeared under the door with a cup of ersatz coffee. Breakfast and lunch together? No matter, it was food. I needed a piss and banged hard on the door. It took some doing, eventually a goon came and agreed to my wants. We had not returned to the cell when another appeared and beckoned me to follow. I fell in behind him, feeling apprehensive. What now? Maybe this was my moment. Still, it was better to be doing something. We walked along a quiet, empty corridor, passing many doors. I wondered what was behind them. Other chaps like me waiting for something to happen? The guard knocked, opened the door and bundled me into a room to face a German officer. He looked to be about my own age, perhaps younger, pleasant, half-smiling, his uniform so smart in comparison with my dirty green-stained brown battledress. That must have puzzled him; he knew I was RAF and should be dressed in blue. He turned behind his desk, gesturing, almost apologetically for something he must do. Wearing a different uniform he would have fitted well into our squadron crowd – perhaps a deliberate ploy.

"Please sit there, Flight Lieutenant," he started, pointing to a comfortable chair. "A cigarette?" He offered me a packet – Players, no less, very impressive. I took one gratefully and his courteous offer of a light, leaning forward to catch the flame. His lighter had been made from a bullet or small cannon shell, very similar to one I'd had in the UK.

He paused, letting me settle. A deep drag – beautiful!

"You understand, of course, we must go through certain formalities here before you can be directed into a POW camp."

Where did this guy get his English? He had a better accent than my own colonial twang!

"First you must complete this Red Cross form. It will be used to tell your family through Geneva, that you are in captivity, safe and well. Your next of kin will be worried for you after receiving the casualty signal from Air Ministry in London saying you were shot down into the Adriatic Sea. It will also mean your name is registered and you can receive food parcels from the Red Cross. Our food here in Germany is rationed. The parcels will be very important when you are in a camp. These two letter cards," he held them up, not letting me take them, "you can use to write to your family. I can have them sent off soon as they are ready."

It sounded great, reassuring and friendly; they had my best interests at heart. I wanted to respond, to thank him for explaining things to me so well, to confess how I had believed it was all going to be so different, the misleading tales I'd been told about interrogation. 'No,' I thought, tapping ash off my cigarette into a small tray made from the base of a shell, gathering my composure, thinking out what to do, 'number, rank and name, that's all.' After all those long dreary travelling days and nightmare nights getting here I felt vulnerable, receptive to his friendly overtures. It was good to be treated so well and in my own language. Half embarrassed, I knew bloody well I wasn't going to give this creep anything at all. He'd only gone through the bullshit they'd told us at OTU. But where to now? Sitting there, a single isolated soul, in a country of millions of hostile Germans on the very brink of defeat. Who knew what they'd get up to?

Would his whole tone change, would he turn aggressive, threatening, have me taken out somewhere. In futile gesture, wanting to do something more than sit there in front of him, saying nothing, unsure, I reached over and took the Red Cross form and the two letter cards.

"Sorry," I said, trying to be courteous, but not allowing too much concession into my voice, "I will give you my number, rank and name, only." How stupid that sounded, I thought, they already had that on my identity card plus more, no doubt, from my first office of interrogation in Fiume. He sat perfectly still looking at me, saying nothing, the silence between us uncomfortable. Methodically, he leaned forward, dragging the shell base of an ask tray towards him, slowly tapping his cigarette on the lip of it. The stillness in the room was getting at me. How long could this go on before I said something? He leaned back in the chair, looking me squarely in the face, saying, "That answer, Flight Lieutenant," a rougher edge to his voice, "I have heard a great many times from British flyers. You have your orders, of course, this I respect, the same way as I have mine, but you must know, this procedure for officers is for your own good." He paused to give that little speech, some weight, "I have explained it is for your family to learn about you, it is necessary for receiving Red Cross parcels," repeating himself, "that is very important for you with our food shortages in Germany. Also we must cover all the procedures before you can join other RAF officers in one of our camps for officer prisoners of war. I must be satisfied with your identification before you can be released from here." That last bit sounded very persuasive, but they had warned that's how it would be spelled out, psychological blackmail, a veiled threat. I felt more confident now that he was following the predicted pattern of interrogation. I held my silence, wondering how long the charade could go on. Was it best not to antagonise the bugger?

He held out 'the latest British bombsight' for me to take in my hands. "You must know about this? We have got complete ones from the bombing raids. It is not as good as the German models, but we know how it works. Other officers have confirmed my knowledge about it."

I refused to take the bomb sight from him, sitting rigid and uncompromising, The more I held my mouth tight closed, the less friendly he became. I hadn't a bloody clue about the bombsight. It was the first I'd ever seen. My ignorance was comforting. He could not extract from me what I did not know. His ignorance of what I may or may know was even more comforting. I stubbed out my cigarette and sat waiting, not looking him in the eye, feigning a disinterested attitude, looking around the room, leaning back.

With relief he ended the interrogation interview in an anticlimax. Without further preamble, his voice sounding tired and disinterested, he said, "Very well, Flight Lieutenant, if that is the way you want to play it. I am sorry for your family in England," waiting to see if I might have a last minute change of heart, not knowing that my family was in Fiji anyway, "go back to your room, I will call you again if I want you." He rose abruptly, walked around the table, flung open the door and called to the guard.

The goon led me back down that long impersonal corridor to my cell. He gave me an encouraging push inside. The bolts shot home, locking me into its isolation. What now? The end or the beginning? I felt unsure about the experience. If thing turned out all right, I had done well; but would things turn out all right? Had they given up on me? I had nothing for them anyway. Besides the damn war was almost over for them. Surely an intelligent chap like that would be more interested in saving his own skin than ordering any harm to an RAF officer. The major chap in Fiume had given me the picture they all knew it was over for them. But what about hostages? Walking back and forth, counting the steps, I tried not to think. I stopped, flopping down on the hard straw palliasse. I tried closing my eyes, forcing sleep; it wouldn't come. I got up again and started the back and forwards routine across the restricted length of bare space, turning sharply, drill square stuff, one, two, three, four, forward; five, six, seven, eight, nine, going on, turning again, on the march, one, two, three, four, until it lost its purpose. What was I doing? Anybody would think I was going bonkers, under immediate threat from a firing squad, or something. I stopped, sitting on the edge of the bed, breathing deeply. 'Control yourself, get a grip' The nothingness of the place weighed heavily. If only someone would bang a door. I tried knocking on the wall. It only thudded, absorbing the bangs of my fist, hurting to do it. No one would hear that, clot! I tried poetry. It would be spring soon, *Oh! To be in England, now that April's there, whoever waits in England*. I'd liked Browning at school. I tried to remember the lines and the rhymes, the flow of words had a soporific effect. I laid down closing my eyes, drifting into the welcome magic of sleep.

I awoke to a noise outside. Suddenly I felt more determined, gritting my teeth. I'd had enough of this bloody circus, they were not going to get me down, all the threats I'd heard were nothing, I had to be more positive in outlook. My change in mind, my determination to push aside everything coincided with the noisy opening of my cell door. A goon stood there, jerking his arm outwards,

"Raus! Raus!" he ordered, telling me to come out, wait in the corridor. What now? What was this one all about?

CHAPTER 17

A Train Journey to Forget

A group of others had already collected there. I joined them. They looked tired, unshaven, dishevelled, dirty, like me. I nodded an acknowledgement at them, silently, receiving only a perfunctory "Hi" in return, nothing more, no one was giving out much in this place.

We were marched off in orderly file, no explanation what it was about. Outside, down the hill to the railway siding, motioned up into a line of waiting cattle trucks, an engine in steam at the head. We were bound for another destination unknown. The sliding doors rasped across, shutting us off from the world at large. It was action of a kind, settling down, finding a space to sit, or stand, an improvement on the isolation of a bare cell; with other people again even if they didn't communicate; some sort of a comfort to be in the presence of others in the same situation.

We were held in suspense, waiting for an interminable hour, sitting, confined by our numbers on the hardness of cold wood, everybody guarded against talking, over cautious, suspicious about spies planted within the truckload. The jerking of the train into movement was a welcome relief. Another stop-start journey into the night, no food, no water, and no warmth. We paused for a pissing stop before complete darkness, guards positioned at intervals, watching, allowing about five minutes.

Back inside, doors slammed shut and fixed, huddling down against the rough, rambling wall, enough space to wrap around oneself, quietly waiting, trying to snatch disturbed sleep, hoping this might be the last journey to POW camp proper. 'What an aspiration,' I thought, 'to be looking forward to being incarcerated behind barbed wire.' Nevertheless, if this journey was to reach a final place it had a welcome kind of purpose.

Capture, and the exhausting pattern of journeys I had taken to get this far, had resulted in my passing into a kind of suspended animation, not feeling anything much, just existing, enduring what had to be endured, grateful for irregular, meagre and inadequate, food. I neither hated, nor accepted my existence; extremes of emotion I could not afford. I simply wanted to survive until the end of the war in one whole piece.

The others around me now, within contact, were not enemies but they were not companions either, just fellow men on the same side as me, going where I was going because they had no choice, accepting this same dreary fate. Our first objective was to survive the journey in the cattle truck and make it to our destination. We all believed that things were going to be easier when we did get there, a forlorn hope; we didn't even know where 'there' might be.

Mid-morning the train stopped; we waited for the restart. It had been going on like that for most of the night. The doors ground back letting in the welcome brightness of daylight.

"Raus! Raus!" We jumped, welcoming the peremptory order to get down from the truck, seeing a massed barbed wire enclosure at a short distance. Thank God! At last, the end of our journey. Falling into an ordered file we moved off with lighter step, tired and hungry but expectant. Somehow the word came down the line, that this was not a final resting-place only a collection and distribution centre organised by POWs. We could expect a short stop to look after our personal needs and 'processing' before finally being sent off to one of the main camps.

It was my first experience, since being shot down, of a place that had been set up to help me. The system seemed like perfection after roaming around Germany in halting drains, dirty, battle-stained and exhausted. First we were directed to a kind of clothing store and issued with forgotten items of personal toilet; razor, soap, toothbrush, towel, comb even a small 'housewife' comprising needle, cotton and buttons. I knew more pleasure in receiving these precious things than from any other gift in my life of living memory! I experienced a real warm glow of delight, a feeling of great luxury, examining each in turn; it felt good just looking at them. They were my own, each one a treasure of possession. Sweeping my tongue over the roughness of my uncleaned teeth I knew great expectations. Someone held his toothbrush high, "Hey! man what is this thing for?" Bloody fool, we laughed at him letting go some of our suppressed pleasure. His kind of humour was infectious. I felt like a human being again, surprised that something so ordinary could generate so much joy.

More was to come. More treats in a bar of chocolate, twenty cigarettes, or a pipe and tobacco. My feeling of wellbeing mounted as I took each with an enthusiastic "Thank you!" Next the sensational thrill of a lifetime, a hot water shower with soap to wash and a towel to dry, a controlled on/off system, but more than enough to rejuvenate me. With typical German precision, the hot water splashed over my grateful body for about forty-five seconds, then, off. But it was a joy to experience again the long forgotten sensuous experience of warm water pouring down on to my head, over my body. I soaped and scrubbed at the accumulated grime, going all the way back to the green dye, still there in places.

Next came a second burst for washing it all off, the same timing of hot again, with a bracing splash of breathless cold to finish. Wonderful! Wonderful! I felt fully refreshed; a new person. Towelling myself dry revealed how much flesh had disappeared from my body. Never a plump person I now had bones protruding where there had previously been ample coverage, I was cleaner than before but very much reduced in weight.

I put on the old clothes again, the heavy soiled flying boots all still faintly tinged in sea marker green. No matter, my body was mine again.

They fed us. Not so much a meal as a feast, small in quantity by any standards but an experience of pleasure after so much less for so long. Each savoured mouthful was almost too good to swallow. The cup of soup had a wonderful flavour, then a small piece of tinned turkey and it wasn't even Christmas, two finger sized slivers of cheese, a half slice of thin black bread, two biscuits and five dried prunes. There was no talk, everyone concentrating on enjoying what had come their way, grinning their pleasure, happy, satisfied with life as it stood. I turned and looked at one of the organisers wanting to say something of my gratitude.

"Bloody marvellous, mate! Thank you very much." A mumble around me gave my appreciation emphasis. "Where does all this stuff come from?"

"It's from Red Cross parcels. You'll see more of that in time when you get to a permanent place – if the trucks that bring it can get through, there's a hell of a lot destruction going on, they can't always make it." He smiled benevolently, knowing what it meant to most of us after the hardships we'd suffered getting here.

I searched out and found a bed space, a straw palliasse on the floor and a rug. My world was complete – for the moment. I was free to wander within the compound wire, to think about where I had come from, those days of nightmare travel out there, and where I might end up. Others sauntering around aimlessly over the bare ground, mostly heads down, showing they did not wish to exchange greetings or welcome any advances of companionship. It puzzled me. I felt good. I wanted to share something with others.

They moved around in twos and threes, maybe crew members who had come in together. I couldn't penetrate any of them. I tried, "Hello there, been here long?" The reactions were either completely blank or a courteous, 'Hello' before walking away. Maybe they suspected my motives; we had been warned in training about enemy spies planted within the camps to gain information. I saw only that men who'd lost their freedom, cooped up and insecure, developed a king of neutral attitude to anyone they did not know. Not defeatism, nor a demonstration of hopelessness behind barbed wire, but just not smiling or friendly, or even receptive. It saddened me. Were we not all part of the same service? Did we not find ourselves in the same predicament? Had we not a stronger need for companionship, a bond of country and cause. I failed to coax any of them from their withdrawal into self-induced isolation.

Perhaps it was the dreariness of our surroundings, the bare wooden huts, the loose dirt of the compound, the block of ablutions with no privacy in any form, one central cookhouse providing our marginal sustenance, that served to block off the fellow feeling I so much wanted to create. We were alone, yet together, with nothing to do in a dreary world yet seemingly unable to enjoy the freedom of human communication available to us. No one wanted to swap experiences despite the fact that they all had a story to tell. If only we could have talked, the dreary daily life would surely have been lightened. I needed to get closer to someone, to feel a companionship yet I failed in every attempt. I felt confused and lonelier still.

The compound had a routine, what else within a German establishment! After waking each day, washing superficially before the first scant meal, something warm to drink: a slice of black bread and maybe some sort of grease or jam, roll call, and then the rest of the day off. Off what? I sometimes wondered. In the evening another small meal, black bread again, soup and another roll call. Occasionally a small 'goodie' like those we had received on arrival

The days dragged on, certain in the knowledge it would be the same again tomorrow, same again the next day, trapped within the confines of the barbed wire cage, a life without real meaning, waiting for that final journey to wherever. I became restless, and realised there had been more distraction in travelling across war torn Germany in the erratic trains, exposed to the dangers of an hostile population and dive bombing and strafing by allied planes. Now we were secure, but our lives were drab, spent wandering around in endless boredom.

The allied armies advance from the beachheads in Normandy, across France and Germany was rapid and unstoppable. We had but to wait out our time, stay in one piece, hope for the best. I wondered whether our own Air Force fighter pilots could mistake our barbed wire enclosures for anything in the enemy lines of defence. We were highly vulnerable to firepower mistakes made from the air.

The days came and went until, without warning, the goons paraded a gaggle of us for entraining and the journey we had hoped for. It took the usual familiar pattern, counting off the numbers at roll call, down the hill in disciplined files of three and clambering up into the waiting cattle trucks. I never knew who or what decided which of us were to be included. Some hidden mechanism somewhere worked it out and coming to my name they said, "Put him on the list."

Shut inside the harsh bareness of the featureless truck, we sat, waiting, patiently, there was no choice about it, until the train jerked into movement. We knew only to travel, to wait and see when the doors opened again, where our journey would end. We travelled the rest of a day and into the night with one pissing stop before dark, no food, no water, just like the last time but with the big difference, so we hoped, of a final destination in this war. On we went, jolting from one stop to the next, cold, numb-bummed. Then came the almost welcome sound.

"Raus! Raus!" the usual order. We tumbled out at the siding, pleased to leave the discomfort of the truck, falling in, in threes, marching expectantly towards the elevated towers in the distance. Somebody said, "It's Stalag Luft Three." To me it meant nothing more than journeys end.

CHAPTER 18

Incarceration

During the twenty-four hours of cattle truck misery I'd found a companion. Bluey had looked at me within the dim light, his conspicuous Royal Australian Air Force, blue battledress, topped by a flash of unruly red hair and a pattern of face freckles. I'd smiled, nodding a greeting thinking we had a common link for friendship, coming from the other side of the world and, as he was to put it, "The cockey's arse tour of Germany to get this far."

"Yer know, mate," he volunteered, "funny to say, I'll be bloody pleased to get into a POW camp. Never thought I'd hear myself, or anyone else, say something like that!"

He was the first to speak freely of his experiences to me. A fighter pilot of sorts, it had taken two weeks after his Beaufighter was hit by flak and downed. Shuffled from one place to another, not knowing 'who was up who or who was paying', as he put it, until now, it was a relief to be going into a proper camp. 'Like reaching the finishing post of a bloody European assault course eh?' His irrepressible Australian wit rising to the occasion, Bluey, never lost for a word, had established a welcome rapport between us. 'Got to keep these Poms happy,' he'd said, to the hearing of those immediately around us. No one reacted.

The encampment was a town of tangled barbed wire, dwarfing anything I'd imagined or seen, its high fences flanking lanes within an outer perimeter, dividing areas of bare earth into compounds. Each had its lines of bare board huts, all within one huge labyrinthine embrace. Men milled around everywhere, seeming to welcome something different to look at. The endless strands of coiled wire stifled freedom in every direction as we marched deeper into its restricting tentacles. At the centre I could see the chain of menacing towers on high stilts, the searchlights and machine guns with their unspoken message.

Every strand in the miles and miles of wire around us had its full quota of prominent pointed barbs, vicious looking little sentinels guarding our perimeters. The days drifted, one after the other, an occasional passing event stirring my lethargy of mind, too many men in too small a space for anything really organised, just a continuous human flow without expansion of size or bed spaces. The numbers seemed to increase with alarming regularity. I lapsed into a listless existence, a kind of mental hibernation.

The story of a cat in our compound generated a welcome diversion. Someone managed to catch it, cook it and eat it without drawing attention within the confined space, an achievement more interesting than the surprising meal, someone's addition to their small twice-daily food ration.

The compound grapevine announced another break in our monotony, an RC Padre had arrived, a Parachute Brigade man waiting near the main gate to hear confessions and to say mass for the Catholics. I went in search of this unusual priest, more in curiosity than intent. He looked a fine man without the customary collar back-to-front, without vestments, ready to offer mass on the stark paleness of a bare wooden table, messenger of God in this place he might have forsaken.

I hesitated, wondering whether I had anything spiritual left in me, but feeling the need to find something, knowing unless I made a real effort it would elude me. I knew I must take the opportunity on offer. If this man could find the energy and faith to travel from camp to camp, compound to compound, he could only be a link into something worth looking for.

I wondered if he could replace my emotional vacuum after all I had endured. I knew full well nothing was easy about my faith but I wanted to give it a go, my mind going all the way back to the blessed nuns encountered in the first few years of my childhood, saying it was a matter of grace, a guardian angel standing on my right shoulder, protection against the devil haunting me on my left side. The years

A cartoon drawn by a fellow POW – Stalag Luft 3, 1945.

in uniform had not sustained any consistent feeling for it, yet I knew beyond any doubt my survival in the war up to this time had been a greater thing than any chance or courage of my own making.

At the moment of communion I closed my eyes with firm intent, took the consecrated host on my tongue, not hoping for a blinding flash or miracle, for a feeling of comfort. 'Be humble and contrite and believe' the nuns had taught us, 'and God will come to you.' Listening to him intoning the blessing I hoped so with all my might,

"*Corpus Domini nostri Jesu Christi custodlat animum tuam in vitan aetemem. Amen.*" The familiar words sounded a strength in my receptive ears, somehow related to the good things of my life, removed and long ago but refreshed in some mysterious way. What I had sought, what I had believed was beyond my contact in this place, had a warmth, a feeling of pleasure to it. Then he ended at the line of men kneeling on the bare ground. The mass was over. He intoned the dismissal, "*Ite missa est.*" We responded "*Deo Gratias.*" Off he went out through our gates to other compounds, sadly no time for talking or consolation, a tireless human link between men and the God they believed in, a man of tremendous character, a true messenger of faith. I looked over the others worshipping with me, not talking, looks of passing contentment on their faces. 'Thank God for religion,' I thought.

I disbelieved my ears, hearing the first booming sound of guns across the humdrum day. Everybody stood still listening, waiting for the next burst. Was it thunder? Were the allies getting close enough for us to hear their heavy artillery? Even if they were German guns it made no difference; they would be firing at the allies from a distance close enough to carry into our compound. How long did that mean for them to reach into our camp, to set us free from the enveloping barbed wire? I prayed that sooner rather than later we would see the men behind those guns marching in, to show us the freedom we yearned for.

But I had not bargained for the tenacity of an almost defeated German nation; the Nazis were not about to give in that easily, they were not yet spent, there was still something to add to the misery of our POW existence. I found Bluey standing at the perimeter fence, listening intently.

"What yer think, mate? Almost time for us to get out of here. Those guys cannot be many miles away. Bloody marvellous, isn't it?" He did not answer, waiting for the next booming sound, hoping.

Spotting the lively compound major who ran our administrative affairs, busy as usual moving around passing a message.

"What about the sound of that major?" I said, excitedly, nodding my head to show expectant pleasure. He did not respond in the way I'd expected.

"We've got to march, Fiji," he said, "I have just had the orders from the camp commandant, every man from every compound is to be on the road in one hour, we have been ordered to move back eastwards away from the advancing army."

I couldn't believe my ears. March out, move back eastwards, the whole bloody shebang?

"What in hell for? Where are we going?"

"Never mind about that, Fiji, you are to be out on the road, forming into the column in sixty minutes – and that's an order."

The man was accepting to do it. A crazy idea. So they wanted us for hostages, moving us back from the advancing allied armies. Out of the sanctuary of our barbed wire city on to the back roads, heading for who knew where, an endless column of emaciated men. It didn't make any sense at all. In numbers of bodies we could easily have swamped them; they were just a bunch of ancient goons carrying obsolete rifles accompanied by a few dogs But, no, that was not to be the way of it.

ONE OF THE GOONS

CHAPTER 19

The Long March

We formed up in hut sized platoons, orderly and disciplined, obeying the commands of those who commanded us who were in turn commanded. Out we went, a long dreary column carrying the only pitiful belongs we owned, physically weak from too little exercise and inadequate food on a journey that was to demand an endurance beyond the reach of many hundreds. It was hard going soon as the novelty of being out in the open again, after being cooped together, had worn off. During our first morning on the road, the routine of stopping every hour for a five-minute break, seemed a waste of time. No sooner had the word travelled down from the leading platoons for a break, the order 'fall in, fall in' seem to follow. Why bother?

As the trudging day wore on, the mood changed and the breaks were a welcome pause until as dusk covered us and the night's halt was called. We sank down, weary, with little interest in preparing a pad in the open for the night. The goons marched at intervals along the fringes of the column, their dogs leashed and panting, also showed signs of the tiredness we felt. Our second day showed there had been desertions in the night. Even the numbers guarding the long column seemed to have been reduced, both soldiers and in dogs. The fifty-five minutes of marching extended in physical demand as the day progress. Each rest halt of five minutes disappeared in a matter of seconds. After a full hour at midday, to eat the mere scraps of food available, we laboured to get up once again on our feet and move.

"Why don't we just stay down, Bluey? They cannot do anything to us. They wouldn't have the guts to shoot us in cold blood. Dozens must have gone last night, even some of the guards and the dogs."

"Nope." He was quite positive. "There's no knowing what might be out there away from the safety of the column. Not much to eat here, I know, but out there could be nothing at all. Too many bloody troops wandering around with guns."

I knew he was right. The retreat was a ridiculous idea but our safety, my safety, my survival to the end rested within the column, not wandering around in a war-wasted countryside full of deserters and all the other menaces of front-line warfare.

We started our day at the end of the week, tired and wet from exposure, the occasional residue of snow here and there to remind us winter had but recently passed. My platoon had progressed to the head of the column for its one-day lead. The major, still his active self, moved up and down the long lines of men, apparently tireless, promising Red Cross parcels not too far away. We had a rendezvous at about twelve hour's march. It lifted our spirits knowing we had no issue of food for that day. The prospect of one of those boxes of goodies boosted my failing spirits.

We had been going for about three hours when the order came for a forced march, right into the night, regardless of the cold drizzle on us, its penetrating wetness enough to dampen the spirits of even the stout hearted. At our final break before dark, the platoon leaders rushed up and down their groups urging us to go. We had something to go for; a Red Cross convoy of trucks.

I was sodden and as despondent as I had been when hauled out of the Adriatic Sea. Every step required a conscious effort. Slipping and limping on the unseen surface of the road, I began to feel the pain of my feet. We went on like zombies into the night.

"You can't stop now mate, the only food we'll get is with those trucks. Come on, you can make it." That night I had much to thank that tough little Australian for.

In the pale light of dawn I noticed there were fewer people in my platoon. My own strength was almost spent. It would be so much easier to just stay down, to go no further. Yet would I survive like that, with no food and without what security we had. Most of the guards had taken off. There were no dogs now. One ancient goon was still with us only because two stout hearted POWS carried his gun for him while he struggled to keep up.

I lay down and put my feet up on a bank to drain the blood from my numb legs. I knew the decision about going on had been made for me. With nothing left, knowing full well I was giving in, I sat there, wet, wretched, ashamed and wondering what might happen now. I said nothing to Bluey who had walked all those dreary kilometres at my side, assisting and encouraging when I needed it. When they got up to go I would remain and hope for the best. Bluey would accept that. I'd been limping for days, the bunched up and wet fleecy lining of my flying boots had slowly worn away at the balls of my feet. The soft flesh could not endure it. Big, angry red blisters had formed, painful, growing worse with every step, now filled with pus and worsening.

Even as I sat, spent and miserable, worrying over being left, a heaven sent respite came down the line. We were resting until midday. The night's rain and wet sky had cleared and low scudding clouds with weak sunshine in between, helped. Easing off each wet boot in turn I looked at my feet, surprised at the extent of infection, wondering how I'd managed to walk on them. Barefooted, I hobbled over to a small stream, fresh from the overnight rain, I took a razor blade from my housewife kit and carefully slit open each repulsive sack of blood and pus, emptying the mess from them into the clear running water, washing each one as clean as I could, leaving an empty blister, tearing off a shirt-tail to wrap around the inflamed area, lessening the pain. I felt the relief instantly, it was still sensitive to touch but I knew I was OK to go on now for a short distance. The act of surgery completed, I risked eating my last morsels of bread, slowly chewing the dampness out of it. Black bread with its wood content lasted well. It took so little food now to satisfy my shrunken stomach.

The days halt was extended into a night's stopover. Bluey and I found a small haystack, carefully spreading a thick layer on the damp ground, piling the straw on either side, stretching out, pulling the pile on top. It made an excellent insulation. Our bodies close for warmth we drifted in and out of sleep right through the night. There was frost on top in the morning but we had gained a vital rest. I had somehow won my struggle to go on when so many others had failed, dropping out; a personal victory made possible by some unknown intervention again. I wondered at it.

Our long column of men had slowly dwindled away. Where they had gone to was anybody's guess. The guards were no longer in real control, many having disappeared. The discipline of our marching retreat was mostly in the hands of people like our major.

The weather was changing, with signs of early spring to lift our tired bodies for the last effort to the Red Cross parcels trucks. Winding down past an open field the column was almost halted by the sight of dancing hares, cavorting through their rituals, racing around, prancing at one another, raising a welcome chuckle from the lines of weary men.

We found mounds of buried potatoes and sugar beet, the former to be roasted and eaten with relish, the sweet taste of the latter eaten greedily. Later, the sight of men's bared arses alongside the line of march proclaimed the misery experienced from gorging raw beet!

Our pace slackened over the day but we knew to keep moving with the word that the longed for Red Cross trucks were only a few miles ahead of us. The splendid word about it passed quickly down the column, one man to another. 'Red Cross parcels, only a few miles to go now'. The expectation putting a spring into every foot marching the country road. We passed into a thickly wooded pine forest, the road through it flanked by a railway siding, a train in steam with a line of trucks clearly visible and taking on water.

We quickened our pace, not wanting to linger near a tempting target like that. We urged, those ahead to move quicker, wanting to get as far as possible from the train. So many in the column had almost come to grief from strafing planes, many escaping death by a mere hairs breadth. There would be flak guns in there somewhere, without a doubt. I felt like pushing everybody forward, running from it, but we were constrained by the slow pace of the platoons up front. I tried to hold down my fears.

The sound of flying engines came to us before we knew it. Two United States Air Force Thunderbolts appeared overhead, roaring across in loose line astern, low down above a broken layer of stratus cloud. They flashed on, out of sight. Perversely, I felt disappointed, thinking they'd missed a the quick as lighting sight of the train stationery in among the pines. They had missed a prime target, thank goodness for us, stupid Americans, no eyes to see what was there for the taking.

How wrongly I judged them. They had spotted it alright. They were circling widely, gaining the height they wanted for a dive bombing and strafing run. We heard their engines fade only to increase in volume again as they lined up, coming back into the attack. The noise level swiftly rose from a distant buzz into a powerful roaring sound, growing ever closer, swooping for that siding and the steaming locomotive. Shouts of alarm sounded along the column trying to be heard above the planes.

"Take cover! Take cover! Down everybody, they're coming at us, DOWN!" The two of them swept in, drowning out the warning calls around me. I bolted in panic going for a small ditch at the side of our road feeling exposed in the widely spaced pine trees.

Two gigantic detonations, almost simultaneous, ripped the world around me wide open, the ground itself seeming to disintegrate beneath me. Every sense of my body was completely overwhelmed, the cacophony of sound bursting in my ears, compressing time and space. The violent force of the bomb blasts pitched me arse over tit like a feather in a whirlwind. I struck the ground hard, knocking the breath from me. I had no sense of time before the second pair of bombs burst, buffeting the air again, tearing the trees apart as I huddled in the ditch. The locomotive exploded in a huge gushing cloud of steam, erupting in the rail siding. Bomb shrapnel and machine gun bullets zipped and smashed, cutting away great chunks of tree bark, bare white pine patches appearing instantly, in, around and over my head. The deadly strikes of metal whined and ricocheted in every direction as cowering, I waited for the next piece of metal to strike. Even as the intensity of the attack died off I felt my flesh creep, still sensitive, waiting to feel a hit, to be killed. The havoc and panic, seemed to continue even after the sound of aero engines had vanished into the distance. Our column of tired and hungry men had been torn apart in mere seconds, almost demolished, left mentally shattered in pain and fear.

When we again became conscious of nothing more than the pungent smell of explosives and the hissing of steam from the fatally wounded locomotive, everybody slowly lifted from the ground, looking around in disbelief. The pine trees had been torn apart, ravaged by a mighty force. We stood in a vacuum, dazed, gazing at one another, wondering at being alive. I checked myself over: nothing broken, no wounds anywhere, every part of me felt intact. It had been such a near thing. I had been at the centre of all that mayhem and emerged undamaged. It was hard to believe my good fortune; a sort of miracle.

It took about half an hour for the dispersed column of men to gather their scattered wits, coming back on to the road, slightly bewildered, snatching at scraps of conversation, shaking their heads, knowing full well what had taken place, wondering at the fact that we were still alive.

The whole nerve-shattering experience had lasted less than a minute, bursting into our midst at shocking speed, blasting at us for only terrible, terrifying seconds, before disappearing again leaving the column in a dazed state of shock. The section leaders called us back onto the road, into line again, walking off, following those in front, pleased to be leaving the plundered railway siding, the smoking debris, the smashed up pine trees. Hurrying into my position in the line I saw white faces of shocked men, clearly showing the effects of living through the attack. Two huge craters were still smouldering, bombed circles of destruction where there had been road surface and pines. Three bodies lay on the ground, half in and half out of the circles of burnt earth, they had been flung into a horrible disarray, red meat and white bones protruding hideously; raw, pink flesh still bleeding. One was still spurting lifeblood, another, just a torso, lay twisted and torn apart.

The sight of those mutilated bodies, so recently alive, part of our long marching column, gore still oozing from them, was too shocking to see. I turned away, horrified by the appalling brutality that had taken their lives so quickly and so mercilessly. Seeing the reality of a dive bombing, strafing attack, the destructive end of it, brought home to me the terrible result I had never seen when flying my operational missions from the squadron. It had always been easy to zoom away, knowing only to make it safely back to base, never having to see the tragedy my bombs and my guns had left behind, the killed and mutilated bodies of an enemy perhaps, but above all human beings who had once lived.

I passed on silently, walking with head down, thinking about what I had been trained to do and how willingly I had done it, wondering how many people I may have killed in the process or how many others I might have crippled or injured. The column trudged on, not speaking, moving along the road silently, still in the shock of their afternoon's experience.

In the fading light of that frightening day we were halted. It was the place for distributing Red Cross boxes. We had walked far, struggling against cold, rain and almost overwhelming fatigue. Now the boxes were to hand, there was no rush, no impatience to get what was our due. I sat on the side of the road for a spell, catching my breath, waiting expectantly. When our turn came Bluey and I went together, feeling good, one box to be shared between two men. It was like a birthday and a Christmas present all rolled into a single container. We knew before opening it that inside were the goodies we had missed for longer than could be remembered, all compactly wedged in, exciting to take out and examine, one item at a time.

Our column major, still lively, came bouncing along the line and stopped to talk.

"How's it going for you now. Feet holding up alright?"

What a marvellous little man! His own trials were no less than ours but with the added burden of organising and keeping the marching men in some kind of discipline for survival. "We're quite close to our destination now, Moosburg, Stalag Seven A. We should

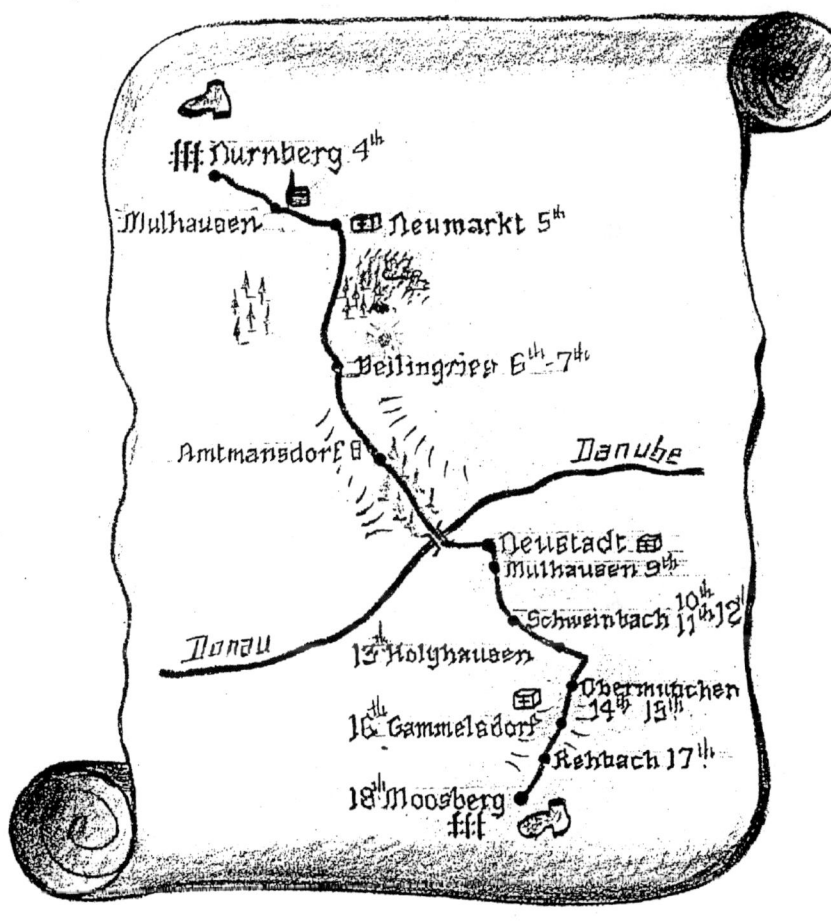

Map drawn by a fellow POW showing the course of our march from Nurnberg to Moosberg in 1945.

be there by tomorrow afternoon. I have heard its a bit of a sardine can already. Too many POWS for the space they have. Still, its our best chance of safety, where kriegies are known to be. After yesterday's attack you've got to admit that's a pretty important thing. Food too. What there is of it. The Americans are advancing fast this way." He gave a flashing smile, full of encouragement.

"Yeah, major, we're OK now. Good to have these boxes, worth all those bloody kilometres." He moved off down the line. Men like that never received decorations but were heroes beyond citations.

Bluey and I started planning what we'd do with the food in the box. How we'd share it out, using some of it to garnish the few remaining potatoes.

It was hard to believe the walking was nearly finished now. I turned to Bluey.

"I didn't think I was going to make it this far. You've been a great help mate."

He shrugged it off embarrassed by my expressed gratitude.

Whatever awaited us, at least now we could stop walking.

"How far, you reckon, we've been on the road?"

"Don't know rightly, mate, well over a hundred. And we've not got there yet! Ask me when we're inside again"

"Hell!" I said "It feels more like five hundred to me!"

Bluey was not big on conversation, his real value a kind of unspoken companionship, a feeling that another chap was there, reliable, trustworthy. We'd gone a long way struggling against misery together. The open road life had toughened both of us, we knew now we could go a long way yet if needs must.

Our destination came into view unexpectedly. As we descended towards a flat plateau, there it was, plain to see below us, rusting barbed wire fences stretching out in all directions, multi-layered, a sight we knew so well but now without any real menace, its purpose no longer an enclosure, preventing us from running away to fight again but more to provide a secure position until the advancing allied armies released us. The excited chattering along the column told everything.

In the long hour over the last distance, our new home took on its real shape. Barbed wire coiled out along the foot of the slope, ugly towers perched commandingly at the corners, goon guards on top with their machine guns and searchlight heads. They must know their time was near, the end of being a soldier on top, the beginning of a new threat to their security. For us it was a welcome journey's end, even if from a distance we saw bodies milling around like a densely packed ant's nest. It looked overcrowded even without us.

In we went, an orderly stream of men swallowed into the wire cage, our freedom of open space out on the road, surrendered to safety of life behind barbed wire. We were pleased to give up our temporary freedom, sure in our conviction that something better lay ahead.

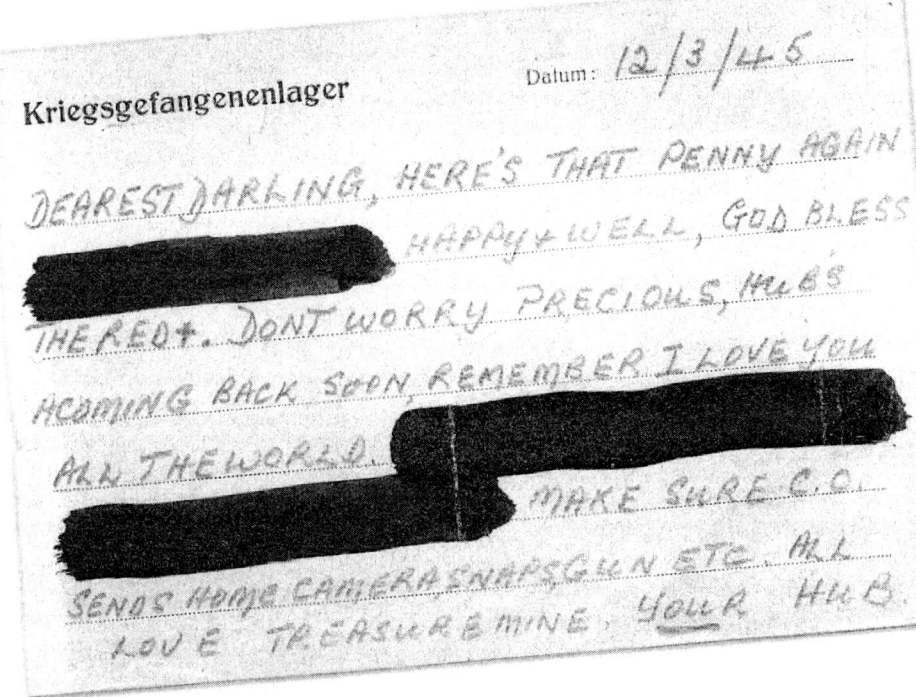

Postcard (heavily censored) sent from Stalag VIIa that landed on my doormat in England four weeks after I had arrived home!

CHAPTER 20

Sweet Freedom

Halting on command like good soldiers we waited patiently to be sorted out and allocated into the endless sprawl of compounds. It took a long time, and a lot of frustrating patience, knowing there were a lot of us to be absorbed.

I wondered at the mass of all these human beings packed together. Everywhere I looked men were milling around. Some looking, some indifferent to our lot. Russian POWs stood staring through the separating fence, zombies, no emotions showing, blank expressions, threadbare clothing, a queer looking lot. Some had lost limbs, hobbling around on one leg propped up by a rough piece of wood, or with empty sleeves, a pitiful sight. There seemed to be thousands of men everywhere you looked, different clothing, different bearing, all concentrated in one vast herd of humans. What kept it so orderly? The huge numbers of men could have overwhelmed anything.

The huts were bursting, three and four tiered bunks, layered ridiculously high, packed close together, almost to the point of being thankful we'd lost so many on the way here; unkind thinking but good practical logic. Bluey, my mate of the march, had disappeared. That relationship had gone. Here it was survival, securing a bunk, learning how the place worked, food, things like that.

Even the bogs were on a queuing system, time allocation by groups of huts. Imagine shitting to order, but we did, waiting our turn for a place in the four rows of concrete seat holes to be vacated, grateful for it. Wherever I sat, wherever I looked, there were lines of bared arses disgorging what little waste the body had processed from a meagre intake of food. I could remember as a youngster watching horses and wondering at their excretions, but here were humans publicly passing waste matter, something we were all accustomed to do in private. These were not normal times; we were not living normal lives. The stench was almost overpowering, worse when the catchment troughs were almost full, waiting to be emptied. It wasn't pleasant; a pattern of life devoid of niceties. There was no choice here. If I wanted to live and survive I knew to take the situation as it came. Nothing could be changed.

Uppermost in every mind in our concentrated mass of bodies was survival. Not survival at any other's cost but survival within the rules of discipline and mutual loyalty. The end was near now and no one spoke it. In all our hearts was the prayer 'please God let me be there at the end.'

The distant pounding of artillery rolled across to us, a message loud and clear, gaining with every passing hour, enlivening our hopeful spirits. The hidden radio set spelled out a message of rescue, saying the allied armies were advancing at great speed, a special advance force had been despatched to take our camp early. An excited grapevine of messages circulated – it had to be soon now – rumour was rife.

We talked about the grand meals to come, the almost forgotten homes left so long ago, what we would do to the gorgeous young females we'd left behind. Our imaginations ran wild while we waited and waited, listening intently for new sounds. The guns were closing, the explosion of their fire telling its own story.

Suddenly everything stopped dead quiet, ears cocked, new sounds were there. First the wild chatter of machine guns, real close, high up on the ridge above our camp, still unsighted, an electrifying effect in the compound.

The staccato gun bursts stirred us into action, men rushing from here to there, searching to see, stopping in groups, restless, talking incessantly, pent up excitement, going from one knot of bodies to another, saying things, not listening much to talk, ears pitched, listening, waiting, hoping.

A new sound came, arresting all movement, fixing attention, the best heard yet, heard from across the hill by the hundreds of us, the unmistakable screeching, grinding noise of tank tracks, a beautiful rumbling. Then the whoomf, whoomf, as they fired, followed by tremendous explosions. The silhouette of a Sherman tank appeared in stark profile on the skyline. We shouted, pointing out the obvious, jumping up and down in a kind of frenzy, like kids at a wild birthday party. It was more than a birthday party, it was wonderful, wonderful, our freedom.

The firing intensified as they encountered unseen resistance, bullets zapping and screaming around us, whacking into the hutment woodwork. Bloody stupid goons trying to put up a fight, to resist against the inevitable! The old dried planks were torn and smashed above my head. I lay flatter on the ground than a sheet of paper. My God! To be hit now when the end was so near!

The sound of several tanks came closer and then they came into view. If my heart had been beating fast at the first sights and sounds it almost burst with joy at the sight. GIs in battle formation came with them, pouring down the hillside, and jeeps with machine guns mounted. The shooting stopped. It was all over. Every person within the wide tangle of enclosing wire stood up and cheered and cheered, wavering arms shouting their joy.

"Hey, here, we're over here!" – "Come on in!" – "Shake you by the hand!"– "Free us!" – "Come on, quickly!" –"Slaughter the bloody krauts!"" No pattern to our yelling, just anything that came into our heads. How would we wait until they burst through the wire.

When the firing had stopped and with the tanks and GIs in full sight, I suddenly realised in that precise moment I was no longer a prisoner of war. I was behind our own allied lines once again. Glory be! Our captors had been captured. The war was over. I was safe, heart bursting with it, thanks be to God! I could not hold back the tears. We hugged one another, burbling sounds of happiness all around. Life was for living again. Soon it could be normal.

In a quieter moment, waiting for the Americans to take over the camp, I thought about the cat that had disappeared from the compound in Nuremberg. It had somehow exhausted its legendary nine lives. How was it then I had escaped so many near misses in my own and was still here. Nothing less than a force beyond my meagre existence had decided my fate.

The Americans entered to wild greetings, a General in his jeep, a pearl handled revolver slung at each hip, stood up waving back at us, acknowledging our appreciation and was gone again. The Red Cross vans, streaming in were besieged; coffee and doughnuts, served by WOMEN, tasted like something from heaven.

Then it all went flat as a pricked balloon, deflated, nothing more to mark the marvellous occasion of being released, no-one else to share my pleasure. Where there should have been celebration there was nothing. It quickly settled into reality. Where there had been scarcity, there was food. Where there had been German masters, the British had taken over. It was not normal but it was a whole lot better, waiting to go home.

The Russians tore down the fences. They found and slaughtered pigs, trading blocks of flesh for cigarettes, four for a hunk of bloody pork.

I was unsure of my feelings after the first flush of joy. The months of captivity and the enduring hardships of survival had blunted my emotions. After months of keen anticipation, the end of the war had now arrived and I felt nothing.

It was to be a slow process back to normality over a long period of time. I was half my weight and only half in control of my mind. The joy of normal living had yet to come…

*The Author, Flt/Lt Dennis McCaig, RAF
on return to England 1945.*